574.5
COL   Collard, Sneed B.

         Alien invaders

DUE DATE	BRODART	05/97	22.00

ALIEN INVADERS

the continuing threat of exotic species

Sneed B. Collard III

A VENTURE BOOK

FRANKLIN WATTS • A Division of Grolier Publishing
New York • London • Hong Kong • Sydney • Danbury, CT

ALIEN INVADERS

the continuing threat of exotic species

For my Aunt Carolyn, whose humor, love, and support never fail

Photographs ©: Sneed B. Collard III: cover, pp. 19, 25, 29, 32, 40, 51, 52, 53, 56, 61, 63, 65, 67, 71, 72, 74, 75, 76, 80, 81, 82, 84, 87, 94 (both photos), 96, 98 bottom, 101, 106, 108, 109 (both photos), 116, 117, 118, 124; Courtesy of Jack Jeffrey: pp. 26, 78; Courtesy of Michigan Sea Grant: pp. 34, 35; Reprinted with special permission of King Features: p. 113; Lisa Nordquist: pp. 14, 15, 20; State Library of New South Wales, Australia: pp. 46, 48; U.S. Department of Agriculture: pp. 37, 91, 98 top; The Far Side © 1991 Farworks, Inc./Dist. of Universal Press Syndicate. Reprinted with permission: p. 38. Courtesy of the U.S. Fish and Wildlife Service, 85

Illustration p. 12: Robert Gillmor

Library of Congress Cataloging-in-Publication Data

Collard, Sneed B.
  Alien invaders: the continuing threat of exotic species /
Sneed B. Collard III.
       p.   cm.— (A Venture book)
  Includes bibliographical references (p.) and index.
  Summary: Explains the problems posed by living
organisms that invade or spread to new places.
  ISBN: 0-531-11298-5
  1. Animal introduction—Juvenile literature. [1. Animal introduction.]
I. Title.
  QL86.C64   I. Title.
  574.5′24—dc20   96-13552   CIP   AC

1 2 3 4 5 6 7 8 9 0 R 05 04 03 02 01 00 99 98 97 96

table of contents

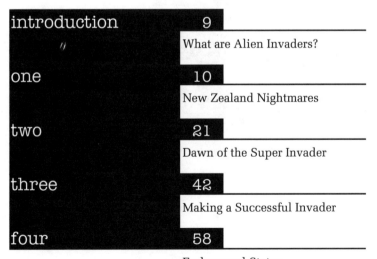

ALIEN INVADERS

the continuing threat of exotic species

Introduction

What Are Alien Invaders?

This book is about living organisms that invade or spread to new places—places where they don't belong. These living things go by many names, such as exotic species, biological invaders, alien species, and nonindigenous species. Thousands of exotic species—including plants, animals, fungi, viruses, and bacteria—have spread throughout the world. According to a 1993 report by the U.S. Congress Office of Technology Assessment, more than 4,500 exotic species have established themselves in the United States alone. Some of these invaders actually help people. Others don't seem to affect things one way or the other. Many invaders, however, have become local, national, and even global disasters. What follows are the stories of the disasters, why they happen, and what we can do about them.

one

New Zealand Nightmares

DISCOVERIES

No place illustrates the problem of biological invasions better than New Zealand. Located in the South Pacific, New Zealand is a group of islands that lie about 2,000 kilometers (1,200 miles) southeast of Australia. The islands were one of the last places on earth to be discovered by human beings. For thousands of years, while people spread out over the rest of the planet, New Zealand remained isolated and uninhabited, protected by the wild southern Pacific Ocean.

Around the year A.D. 800, however, several large sailing canoes cast off from another group of South Pacific islands far to the east. The canoes were filled with Polynesian people looking for a new place to live. No one is sure why the Polynesians left their own homes. Perhaps their islands became overcrowded, with too many people and not enough food. Whatever the reason, a few of the Polynesians decided to brave the open ocean.

The Polynesians were excellent sailors with a tradition of making long ocean voyages. But historians believe that on this voyage, the Polynesians traveled farther than even they had planned. They sailed thousands of miles west and then were caught in a terrible storm. The storm blew them south to a place that they named Aotearoa, or "the Land of the Long White Cloud." Today, we call it New Zealand.

The Polynesians, or Maoris as they are now known, were the first people ever to visit New Zealand. What they found was breathtaking. Dense forests blanketed 80 percent of the country. Three-thousand-meter (10,000-foot) peaks ran like giant backbones down the centers of New Zealand's two major islands, North Island and South Island. Volcanoes spit lava and steam like hot breath from deep inside the earth.

Even more fantastic than all this were the animals, many of which were found nowhere else on earth. Some of these animals were ancient forms. They had lived in New Zealand since the islands had been part of the ancient supercontinent Gondwanaland millions of years before. Other animals were relative newcomers. They had arrived by flying, floating, or swimming to the islands.

An important feature of this animal life was that it did not include mammalian predators. Mammals appeared on earth only after New Zealand had drifted away from the rest of Gondwanaland. The only mammal that had reached New Zealand was a kind of bat that had flown to the islands. Without mammals to eat them, New Zealand's wildlife had evolved into an incredible variety of forms. The strangest, by far, were the flightless birds. They included flightless geese, parrots, rails, and a dozen kinds of giants called moas.

The Maoris had never seen anything like these birds. The smallest moas stood almost one meter (3 ft.)

Large flightless birds called moas roamed through New Zealand's forests before the arrival of humans.

tall and weighed 22 kilograms (50 lbs.). The biggest towered 4 meters (12 ft.) high and weighed 270 kilograms (600 lbs.)!

Remarkably, many of New Zealand's birds had never learned to defend themselves. With no hungry mammals roaming around, most of New Zealand's wildlife had evolved to "live and let live." This made them easy targets for Maori hunters.

A DEVASTATING FEAST

By the year A.D. 1200, tribes of Maori moa-hunters roamed over many parts of New Zealand. These tribes learned to trap and spear large moas in swamps and bogs. They also gathered the moas' football-size eggs to eat. Unfortunately, the Maoris killed the moas faster than they could reproduce. During the next several hundred years, the populations of moas and many other birds steadily declined as a result of overhunting and egg-gathering.

The Maoris' impact on wildlife was not limited to hunting. They also lit fires that sometimes spread out of control. These fires burned entire forests, which the moas and other birds needed to survive. Once the forests were gone, many of them never grew back.

To make matters worse, the Maoris had brought a companion with them on their original voyage to New Zealand. This companion was the Polynesian rat, called the *kiore*. The Maoris considered the kiore a delicacy, but the rat was not content to hang around Maori villages. The kiore ate almost anything, and it found a sumptuous feast in New Zealand's pristine environment. Seabirds nested by the millions along New Zealand's shores, and their eggs made fine meals for the kiore. So did the chicks of moas and other birds. Giant snails and cricket-like insects called *wetas* offered a tasty treat, as did the slow-moving, lizard-like tuatara.

Between the Maoris and the kiore, New Zealand's wildlife suffered devastating losses. By the time English explorer Captain James Cook arrived in the year 1769, 32 species of New Zealand's large birds had become extinct, including all 12 species of moas. The tuatara and several small birds were also wiped from New Zealand's main islands, and the populations of many other species, including the giant snails, crashed. For other animals, the worst was yet to come.

*The tuatara is a unique reptile found only in
New Zealand. The Polynesian rat, or kiore, exterminated
the tuatara from New Zealand's main islands.
Today, the tuatara manages to survive on
several smaller, rat-free islands.*

THE EUROPEANS

Captain Cook was the first European to really explore
New Zealand. Cook made three visits to the Land of
the Long White Cloud, and after him, a stream of ships
began visiting the islands. Most early Europeans hunted
seals and whales for their skins and blubber. Later,
gold strikes lured thousands of miners into the wilder-
ness while lumbermen began felling giant kauri trees,
the finest shipbuilding trees the world had ever seen.

European settlers used wood from giant kauri trees to build ships. Within a century, 98 percent of the kauri forests were cut down or burned, destroying the homes for many native species.

Proud, fierce warriors, the Maoris fought the European invasion of their lands. In 1840, however, Maori chiefs signed a treaty with the British. The treaty recognized the Maoris' legal rights, but it also made New Zealand a British colony. The treaty opened the door for many European settlers, and European cities and towns soon sprouted up all over New Zealand.

Despite the treaty, the arrival of European settlers did not leave the Maoris or wildlife untouched. Settlers accidentally infected the Maori population with exotic diseases from Europe, including dysentery, tuberculosis, influenza, whooping cough, and measles. The Maoris had little natural resistance to these diseases. From the time the diseases were introduced until well into the twentieth century, they took a horrible toll. The flu epidemic of 1918, for example, killed 2,160 Maoris, a death rate seven times higher than that for European settlers. Diseases also kept Maori infant mortality rates consistently high.

The European settlers also had a profound effect on wildlife. Miners and explorers living in "the bush" shot enormous numbers of native quail and pigeons for food; this was an easy task because these animals had still not learned to fly away or defend themselves. Logging also destroyed the homes of countless native species. But the exotic animals and plants that the Europeans brought with them were perhaps the most dangerous threats to New Zealand wildlife.

DEADLY STOWAWAYS

Rats and cats were the first exotic species to accompany Europeans to New Zealand's shores. Rats were stowaways on almost all ships and traveled wherever seamen went. As soon as European vessels docked at

New Zealand ports, the rodents jumped ship and quickly spread throughout the islands. Two kinds of rats invaded New Zealand. The first was the Norway rat. Like the kiore, the Norway rat ate everything it could sink its teeth into, including bird eggs and chicks, large snails, and a host of insects.

The Norway rat was soon followed by the ship, or black, rat. Black rats were even fiercer than Norway rats and quickly replaced them. Unlike Norway rats, black rats also climbed trees. Up until about 1860, New Zealand's tree-nesting birds had survived fairly well by staying out of reach of people, cats, and rats. But with its squirrel-like climbing abilities, the black rat took its voracious appetite to the highest tree branches and added perching birds to its menu.

Cats also learned that New Zealand animals were easy prey. The first cat conqueror arrived with Captain Cook, and after that, a steady flow of felines went on permanent shore leave. At first, cats remained around towns, but after the year 1870 or so, the predators "went bush." In the forests, cats pounced on native lizards, insects, and ground-dwelling birds. On one offshore island, a lighthouse keeper's cat single-pawedly began a killing spree that wiped out 13 species of birds, including one species that only lived on that island.

Danger to native wildlife did not stop with rats and cats. Millions of exotic sheep and cattle overgrazed and trampled New Zealand's landscapes. This led to soil erosion, which silted up streams and rivers that were home to native fish.

To help them feel more at home in their new country, Europeans also set up *Acclimatization Societies*, which imported thousands more exotic plants and animals from England and other parts of Europe into

New Zealand. Between the 1850s and the early 1900s, Acclimatization Societies imported at least 130 species of birds, 51 species of mammals, 40 species of earthworms, 60 species of spiders and mites, 12 species of slugs and snails, 1,100 species of insects, and more than 1,700 species of flowering plants. Not all of these survived, but many did, including 36 species of exotic birds and 33 species of mammals.

Some of these aliens, such as the rabbit, rampaged out of control and began gobbling up sheep pastures (see also chapter 3). Panicked farmers and ranchers responded by forcing the government to import even more exotic species to get rid of the rabbits. The new invaders included stoats, weasels, and ferrets. These predators ate a few rabbits, but they discovered that New Zealand birds and other animals were much easier to catch. Until the late 1800s, many of the most vulnerable native birds had still survived in remote forests, but now their time came, too. Under pressure from the stoat and its friends, these bird populations also crashed, adding yet more names to New Zealand's list of extinct species. Meanwhile, the rabbits continued to devour pastures, driving many farmers and sheep ranchers to financial ruin.

A TERRIBLE TOTAL

For both Maoris and Europeans, New Zealand offered a land rich in natural resources. The country's forests, rivers, mountains, and animal life helped millions of people survive and prosper.

During the past 1,200 years, however, people and the other invaders they brought inflicted severe and permanent changes to New Zealand's environment. Besides the costs to human health and happiness, the toll on New Zealand's wildlife has been especially

*Cats have been one of the world's most destructive
exotic species. In New Zealand and elsewhere, feral cats have
preyed on and wiped out countless native bird populations.*

devastating. Fifty-five species of birds were driven to extinction or drastically reduced in numbers. So were many native reptiles, insects, and other creatures. Some of these animals survived on smaller offshore islands, but most were lost forever. Large tracts of New Zealand's forests were also destroyed, together with thousands of acres of valuable farmland.

To be fair, neither the Maoris nor Europeans are wholly to blame for the destruction they caused. They did not have our understanding of biology and could not possibly predict the results all their actions would

New Zealand's capital city of Wellington offers beautiful scenery, but two hundred years of biological invaders have left the country biologically poorer than the land that Europeans first encountered.

bring. At the same time, New Zealand's experience highlights some important points about biological invasions around the world. First, biological invasions are not a new phenomenon. They have been happening for thousands of years. Second, most biological invasions do not happen by themselves. As the following chapters more fully explain, almost all modern invasions are caused by the actions of a single species, *Homo sapiens.*

two

Dawn of the Super Invader

New Zealand's history is a clear example of how bio-logical invasions can lead to human suffering, eco-nomic hardship, extinction of species, and damage to the environment. Scientists, in fact, consider biologi-cal invasions to be one of our three most urgent envi-ronmental problems. (The other two are pollution and mismanagement of our natural resources.) This sur-prises many people. After all, living things have been spreading out over our planet since life first appeared on earth more than three billion years ago. This expan-sion is a basic, natural quality of life and is a key to how species survive over time. Why, then, are biologi-cal invasions suddenly such a threat?

A FRIGHTENING FLOOD

The problem with the recent spread of living things is that they are happening at a rate never before wit-nessed on earth. Before historical times, biological invasions happened infrequently, maybe once every several thousand years or so. When an exotic species did enter a new territory or ecosystem, native plants and animals usually had time to adjust to the newcomer. The new species may have driven some local plants and animals to extinction and caused other changes, but ecosystems as a whole probably suffered little damage. This is not true today.

How Long Does it Take to "Go Native?"

One question many people wonder about is how long it takes for an exotic species to be considered a native species. A year? Ten years? A thousand?

Unfortunately, there is no definite rule of thumb for "becoming" a native species. A lot depends on human memories and historical records. In general, species that are known to have invaded new areas because of some kind of human activities are considered to be exotic or alien species (see chapter 3). Those that have reached an area through natural means or events are considered to be native.

In many cases, however, an invader has been in a place for so long that it doesn't seem accurate to keep calling it an exotic species. In these cases, scientists often refer to the species as a *naturalized* species—one that has settled in to become a part of its new home. The Polynesian rat, or kiore, that the Maoris brought to New Zealand (see chapter 1) is a good example of an animal that can be considered naturalized. By the time Europeans arrived in New Zealand, the kiore had been there so long it had become a part of New Zealand's fauna.

What about the Maori people themselves? Compared to New Zealand's native flora and fauna, Maoris are newcomers and are, therefore, aliens. Yet, over hundreds of years Maoris became naturalized, a part of the islands' identity. What's more, Maoris are definitely native if you compare them to Europeans who arrived later. So how do we refer to them?

Scientists will probably never come up with a perfect way to classify human migrants and other unclear cases. On the other hand, a perfect classification system may not be so important. Most modern biological invaders, including those that cause problems, are clearly exotic species and should not be living in their new homes. The important issue is not what we call them, but how we slow them down and limit the damage they cause.

Since human civilizations began popping up on the planet, the rate of exotic species invasions has swelled from a tiny trickle to an overwhelming flood. Like those that happened in New Zealand, almost all recent biological invasions are the direct result of human activities. *Homo sapiens* is without question the Super Invader of all time, and our actions have made it possible for thousands of other invaders to spread over the planet.

Human activities lead to biological invasions in many ways. The first human-caused invasions probably resulted from changes early humans made to the environment. These changes are known as *habitat disturbances*. As early as 40,000 years ago, people in Europe, the Middle East, and North Africa changed their environment by setting fire to brush and wooded areas. The fires helped create pastures for the wild animals that the people liked to hunt. By about 8,000 years ago, humans were also clearing large tracts of natural brush and forests to plant crops and provide grass for domestic grazing animals. When early humans burned or cleared away natural vegetation, they also paved the way for a host of plants that could not live in those areas before.

What were the early invaders like? Most were grasses and other weeds that sprouted quickly and grew well in the sunny pastures and fields people had made. The plants reached their new homes as seeds, often carried by the wind or stuck to the fur of deer, goats, and other grazing animals. These early aliens probably did not travel very far at any one time. They leapfrogged from clearing to clearing, expanding their ranges as people expanded theirs. Alien insects, birds, and other animals followed the weedy plants from place to place.

As agriculture became more sophisticated and early trade grew, the number of plant and animal invasions increased. With the development of shipping and overland trade routes, people purposely began carrying seeds of desirable plants long distances. Barley, a native of southern Europe and the Near East, showed up in Egypt as long as 7,000 years ago. It may have been the first crop ever planted there and was probably traded throughout the Mediterranean region. Fruits, fibers, and other agricultural products were also traded.

Most of the crop plants presented few problems in their new homes. They hung around fields and gardens where they were planted. Mixed in with the desirable seeds, however, were a number of seeds of weed species that were accidentally transported.

*Deer, goats, and other grazing animals probably spread
the seeds of invading weeds as early humans
cleared land for pastures and farms.*

Many of these became pests. In what is now Poland, for example, at least 140 species of plant invaders became permanently established as a result of human activities before the year A.D. 1500.

Animals continued to accompany the plant invaders. Rodents, geckos, cockroaches, and beetles found their way directly onto caravans and ships. Other animals were unknowingly transported in farm and timber products. Without historical records, it's hard to know the impacts of most of these early invaders. Some undoubtedly caused real problems, but the effects of most were probably limited. The invasions, though, had just begun.

Rats: Our Deadly Companions

Rats were probably one of the earliest stowaways to accompany people as we began spreading over the earth and invading new territories. Rats originated in Asia. There are more than 40 species, but only two have hitchhiked with us in large numbers. One is the black rat, *Rattus rattus*, also known as the roof or ship rat. The other is the Norway or brown rat, *Rattus norvegicus*.

In New Zealand and countless other places, these two rodents have an extensive record of escaping into the environment and harming native plants and animals. Rats have also had an enormous impact on human history.

The black rat is perhaps best known for its role in the horrific plagues of the past three thousand years. Plagues, such as bubonic plague, are caused by bacteria that live and grow in

Rats have invaded almost every place humans have settled. They have been responsible for devouring many native species and have spread deadly diseases, such as the bubonic plague.

many kinds of mammals, including rats. Plague is transmitted to humans by the biting fleas that make their homes in the rat's thick fur.

The earliest known plague is recorded in the Bible as happening about the year 1080 B.C. Later plagues rocked Egyptian, Greek, Roman, and other civilizations, wreaking death and destruction on an unimaginable scale. Plagues toppled empires, defeated armies, and depopulated entire regions. The most famous plague, the Black Death, ravaged Europe, Asia, and Africa for three centuries beginning about the year 1340. This *pandemic* claimed more than seventy-five million human lives.

Plague still exists today. It resides mostly in populations of wild animals, but is still commonly transmitted to people. In 1993, 2,065 cases, including 191 fatalities, were reported in ten countries. Most of these cases occurred in Africa and Asia, but plague was also reported in Peru and the United States. Modern pest control efforts help keep plague from spreading from wild animals to urban-dwelling rats. But the potential for new outbreaks always looms, especially in crowded areas with poor sanitation and living conditions.

Colonial contamination

The sixteenth century opened the greatest period of exploration in human history. The voyages of Columbus, Magellan, and later explorers had an unprecedented impact on the spread of exotic species. Ships now linked the New and Old Worlds for the first time since the continents had been connected tens of thousands of years before. Intercontinental travel was here to stay, and plants, animals, and other organisms wasted no time in booking their passage.

Trade continued to be one of the primary activities of early European explorers. Trade goods included jewelry, cloth, cookware, and, of course, agricultural products. Among the agricultural products were species that Europeans were happy to offer, sometimes without the knowledge of native peoples. As early as 1773, for instance, Captain Cook released pigs and goats in New Zealand in an effort to stock the islands with meat. Spices and crop plants were also given to native peoples.

Though Cook's intentions were good, the results of his activities and others like them were mixed. Goats and pigs later caused widespread damage to rain forests and other fragile ecosystems throughout the South Pacific. Crop plants probably benefited natives and explorers alike, but many accidental weed and animal stowaways escaped to become major pests.

Other harmful invaders in the form of diseases spread from European explorers and missionaries to indigenous populations. These epidemics were particularly devastating because native peoples usually had no natural resistance to them. Smallpox, measles, malaria, syphilis—even such seemingly harmless diseases as chicken pox and the flu—swept through native populations with horrifying results. Central Mexico, for example, was home to more than twenty-five million Native Americans when Spanish explorers first arrived in the 1500s. In just four years, from 1520 to 1524, smallpox killed more than three-quarters of the region's population. Measles followed closely behind smallpox, claiming millions more victims.

Early Spanish missionaries constructed missions like this one in Santa Barbara, California, to help establish Spanish claims on North America. Unfortunately, the missionaries also introduced exotic diseases that proved deadly to Native Americans.

SETTLING IN

By the 1600s, European colonial powers had put down roots around the globe, from Chile to California, from South Africa to India. With colonization, the numbers of biological invasions escalated worldwide. As in New Zealand, Acclimatization Societies played an important role in introducing exotic mammals, birds, and ornamental plants to help colonists feel more at home in their new lands. Colonists brought other species for economic reasons. Many food crops now grown in North America, for example, were originally brought from Europe. Trees for timber, fish for sport, and birds for food and hunting were also introduced. In many cases, these introductions were not necessary. Perfectly suitable native species existed in most colonies. Colonists, however, had a poor understanding of local plants and animals and, often, even a fear of them. They preferred to surround themselves with familiar species.

As the numbers of exotic species multiplied, so did the problems they caused. Frequently, species escaped into surrounding environments where they wreaked havoc. In 1889, cattle were introduced into sub-Saharan Africa to feed the Italian Army that was stationed there. The cattle brought with them a disease called rinderpest, which spread to native mammals and killed up to 90 percent of the buffalo, antelopes, and other wild grazing animals in some places. In North America, a seemingly harmless European plant called purple loosestrife was imported at the turn of the nineteenth century. The plant infested wetland areas in 41 states and Canada. It displaced native plants and destroyed the habitats for countless birds.

A few people noticed the negative effects of such introductions and tried to sound the alarm. Early conservationist Sir Walter Lowry Buller, for example, steadfastly opposed the introduction of weasels, stoats, and ferrets to get rid of rabbits in New Zealand. His voice, like many others, was drowned in the search for quick-fix solutions to the colonists' problems.

MODERN MANIA

One might think that as people's understanding of the natural world increased, biological invasions would decrease. In some cases, this has happened. The Federal

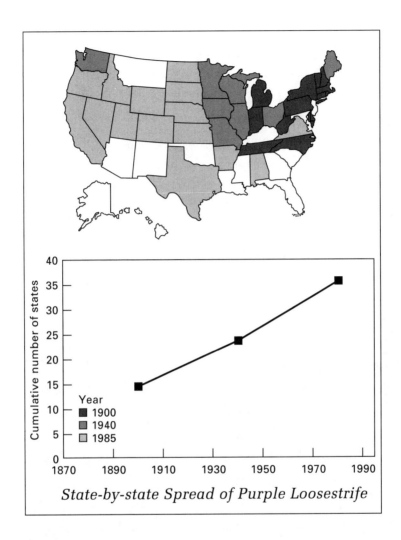

State-by-state Spread of Purple Loosestrife

Seed Act of 1939, for instance, helped reduce the spread of some weeds into the United States. The act accomplished this by requiring that seed imports be free of contamination by the seeds of harmful exotic plants. Unfortunately, successes such as this have been the exception rather than the rule. In many cases, exotic species invasions around the globe have continued or have actually increased.

In 1993, the U.S. Congress Office of Technology Assessment (OTA) released a special report on biological invasions titled *Harmful Non-Indigenous Species in the United States.* Among other things, the OTA report examined why biological invasions keep happening. The report cited a variety of reasons for continuing invasions, all of them tied to human activity.

World trade is still a major culprit. Not only is the volume of international trade increasing, but trading patterns are also changing. Commerce between North America and Asia, for instance, has boomed in the

Commercial airlines are only one of the many modern modes of transportation that help spread biological invaders.

past 50 years, partly as a result of increased immigration of Asians to California. This has led to growing imports of Asian foods and, with them, more opportunities for alien stowaways.

Modern modes of transportation add to the problem. Airplanes are a well-recognized way for exotic species to get from place to place. Ship's ballast is another. Ballast is any heavy material that is loaded into a ship to help stabilize it, especially when the ship is empty. Ballast can include everything from dirt and cement blocks to water. It is often taken in at a ship's point of origin and dumped at its destination. Unfortunately, this practice provides a first-class ticket for alien species. One recent study of ships arriving in Oregon from Japan found at least 367 different kinds of plants and animals in ballast water. Since 1980 alone, ballast water has allowed at least eight new pest species to invade American waters.

Zebra Mussel Madness

The zebra mussel sends the strongest warning yet of the dangers of ship ballast in the spread of exotic species. The pistachio-sized, striped mussel is a native of southern Russia. Over the past 200 years, it has invaded Europe's rivers and lakes, and in the mid-1980s it began its assault on North America.

The first live zebra mussel migrant was collected in 1988. It was found in Lake St. Clair near Detroit, Michigan. Within six years, the mussels had spread to all of the Great Lakes, eight major North American river systems, and countless other bodies of fresh water. Researchers agree that the free-swimming larvae of the zebra mussel arrived in North America in the ballast water of a cargo ship. When this water was dumped into Lake St. Clair, the larvae attached themselves to rocks or other hard surfaces and grew into adult mussels.

Like many biological invaders, the zebra mussel has a tremendous ability to reproduce. Up to two million zebra mussel larvae have been found in a cubic meter of water. They quickly cover almost every available hard surface, including the bottoms of ships, which help carry them from place to place.

The zebra mussel provides some benefits to people. Mussels filter tremendous quantities of water and can help clean up polluted lakes and rivers. They also are very sensitive to certain kinds of pollution. Scientists are testing their use as a *bioindicator species* to help monitor the health of lakes and rivers. The mussel's drawbacks, however, far outweigh its advantages.

Zebra mussels were brought to the U.S. in the ballast of ships.

One of the zebra mussel's most noticeable impacts is that it clogs pipes of power plants and water utilities. The mussel grows in densities of up to 700,000 per square meter (about 75,000 per square foot) and can completely pave over pipes and gratings. Power plants and water utilities must continually scrape, poison, and blast away mussels to prevent them from interfering with water-cooled generators and drinking supplies.

Scientists also fear that zebra mussels are starving other animals by gobbling up all the available food in lakes and streams. This could ruin both sport and commercial fishing industries and drive many other aquatic species to extinction. The mussel already threatens North America's native shellfish. Mussels quickly coat the shells of freshwater clams and oysters, suffocating the animals. In Lake St. Clair, where the zebra mussel was first located, it has already exterminated 18 species of native clams. Hundreds of other native shellfish

Billions of dollars are being spent to clean zebra mussels from boat hulls, sewer pipes, and power company intakes.

species are threatened throughout the continent.

The U.S. Fish and Wildlife Service estimates that in the Great Lakes alone the mussel will cost utilities, industry, and outdoor enthusiasts a total of five billion dollars by the year 2000. So far, researchers have found no efficient way to control the mussels. Hot water, electricity, chlorine and other chemicals—even sound—have been tried. All methods are expensive and many, such as chemicals, damage the environment. The search continues as the striped menace continues to spread.

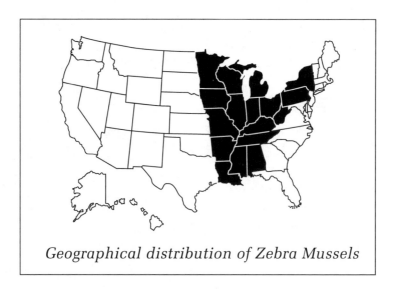

Geographical distribution of Zebra Mussels

Other common invasion pathways are described in the box on page 37. From these descriptions, it is clear that the opportunities for exotic species to invade and cause problems are greater than ever.

Ironically, biological invasions are often given low priority among environmental concerns. Why? According to biologist Warren Herb Wagner, Jr., of the University of Michigan, "Scientists and even non-scientists sometimes argue that the phenomenon of

Common Invasion Pathways

Invaders find their way into North America by many means. Here are four common invasion pathways:

1. MILITARY CARGO

Especially during times of war, the transportation of military cargo has resulted in several biological invasions. These include the golden nematode worm, a serious agricultural pest in North America, and the brown tree snake, which has devastated wildlife on Guam (see chapter 4). Many biologists fear that the heavy air and ship traffic between the United States and the Middle East during Operation Desert Storm (1990–91) may have imported additional invaders.

2. CANALS

Man-made canals have allowed dozens of species to expand their ranges. Between the years 1869 and 1985, at least 41 species of fish invaded the Mediterranean from

Military transportation has been responsible for carrying a number of biological invaders. This tank is being inspected for exotic hitchhikers.

the Red Sea through the Suez Canal, and the rate of invasions appears to be increasing. Canals between the Great Lakes allowed the spread of at least 30 invaders between 1960 and 1990, including the sea lamprey, a fish predator that contributed to the decline of several important fisheries species, such as the lake trout, burbot, and large whitefish.

3. COMMERCIAL SHIPPING

The Asian tiger mosquito is one of hundreds of exotic species that has traveled on commercial cargo ships. In 1985, the mosquito was brought to the United States in a shipment of used tires from Japan. Larvae of the mosquito apparently survived in water in the tires and hatched once they reached American shores. Between 1985 and 1993, the mosquito spread to 351 counties in 24 states. The insect is a fierce biter and transmits such serious diseases as dengue fever, yellow fever, and eastern equine encephalitis (EEE). In 1991, scientists confirmed for the first time that the Asian tiger mosquito was carrying EEE in Florida. In the same year, an outbreak of the disease killed at least two people in the Southeast.

How poodles first came to North America

4. THE PET AND WILDLIFE TRADE

In the U.S., pet industry lobbyists have firmly opposed any restrictions on fish and wildlife imports. Wildlife imports, usually brought in by airplane, generate hundreds of millions of dollars in profits to those involved. In 1994 alone, more than 106 million live fish were legally brought into the United States, mostly for the aquarium trade. Other wildlife imports included:

1,600,000 amphibians
57,000 birds
460,000 corals
1,800,000 insects
96,000 spiders
54,000 mammals
440,000 snails and other mollusks
1,400,000 reptiles

A number of animals imported as pets have already escaped to become pests (see chapters 3 and 4). As the volume of imports grows, we are likely to see many more invasions in the future.

invasives is not at all new, but simply a human-induced variation on an ancient theme."[1] For this reason, they are ignored by some scientists and public officials, despite the severe harm that biological invasions cause.

Another reason people pay little attention to biological invasions is because they happen gradually compared to other crises. According to the OTA report, "One expert estimates that non-indigenous weeds usually have been in the country for 30 years or

*Air pollution and other obvious environmental hazards
are easier to recognize and usually receive more
attention than biological invasions.*

have spread to 10,000 acres before they are detected."[2] By the time people recognize an invasion, it is often too advanced, difficult, and costly to deal with.

A third reason biological invasions are often overlooked is that they don't seem as urgent as other environmental problems, such as acid rain, damage to the ozone layer, and global warming. Except for a few well-publicized cases, such as killer or African bees (see chapter 4), invaders haven't been good at capturing headlines or generating action. Fish and wildlife biologist Bruce Coblentz of Oregon State University explains, "Environmental concerns having to do with resource use and pollution are foremost in our minds and are pre-eminent in the media. In most cases problems in these two categories are among the most acute, and most directly affect human welfare."[3]

Nonetheless, the consequences of biological invasions grow every year, and unlike many other problems they are often permanent. Can the invaders be stopped or at least slowed down? To answer that question, it helps to understand what makes an invader successful.

three

Making a Successful Invader

Despite the tremendous damage that they cause, only a small percentage of exotic species actually make successful invaders. One scientist estimated that out of every one hundred exotic species arriving on foreign shores, only two or three spread into their new environments. This does not make biological invaders any less of a problem, because the invaders that are successful often cause great harm and suffering. By understanding what makes certain invaders successful, however, we can learn a lot about stopping future invasions and controlling those already underway.

Biologists have spent a lot of time and effort trying to figure out what makes some invaders so bad. After 70 years of study, about the only thing that most scientists agree on is that rules are hard to come by. One researcher, who was trying to reach conclusions about insect invasions, complained, "It is depressing to be unable to draw striking generalizations about introduced insects but it would serve no worthwhile purpose...."[1] Another scientist stated, "We are finding that [rules] are often so trivial as to be useless, or they are simply wrong."[2]

Nevertheless, the success an exotic species has invading a new habitat seems to depend on three factors:

1. the qualities or traits of the invader

2. the conditions of the place being invaded

3. the ability of the invader to reach a new place or site from its original home.

An account of the European rabbit in Australia shows what can happen when all of these pieces come together.

DOING THE BUNNY HOP

The story of the European rabbit in Australia began with the colonization of Australia near the close of the eighteenth century. When English colonists arrived Down Under, they discovered a strange and often hostile world. Australia's native aborigines were unlike anyone the Europeans had ever seen. The same was true of Australia's wildlife. Unlike Europe, the southern continent was filled with a bizarre collection of kangaroos, wallabies, and other pouched mammals called *marsupials*. Some of these could be hunted for meat or fur, but most were considered ugly vermin by the colonists. What the English settlers really desired were animals they were familiar with.

Enter the rabbit.

Bringing the rabbit to Australia must have seemed like the perfect solution to many of the colonists' problems. If rabbits could be established Down Under, they could be used for food, fur, and even sport. To top it off, rabbits were soft and fuzzy and provided the colonists with comforting reminders of their homes in England.

Almost from the day it began being colonized, Australia was the site of numerous attempts to introduce the rabbit into the wild. The first rabbits probably arrived in Australia with the English First Fleet in 1788. Five of the creatures, together with an assortment of livestock, were brought to help feed the population of the fledgling colony. A second group of rabbits arrived three years later. Neither of these groups was well-protected, and neither fared well on the southern continent. Dogs, dingoes, snakes, and other predators made quick work of the rabbits, but this did not deter people from bringing more.

In attempts to make their country more rabbit-friendly, farmers and sportsmen started going to great lengths to protect the furry creatures. Some landowners built elaborate stone and earth homes to shield the rabbits from predators. Others poisoned dingoes, eagles, kangaroos, wombats, and other native animals that might bother the rabbits. Eventually, human efforts bore fruit.

The breakthrough most likely came in 1859, courtesy of a wealthy English tenant-farmer named Thomas Austin. Austin lived in the state of Victoria, and he fancied himself quite the sportsman. He imported partridges, hares, and rabbits to provide scenery and hunting opportunities for his friends and himself. To ensure the animals' success, Austin built protected paddocks for the animals to live in and even hired a gamekeeper to kill any hawks and eagles that might be lurking about.

How Austin's rabbits actually escaped into the wild is unclear. Austin may have released 13 of them soon after they arrived. Another possibility is that a high flood may have freed the rabbits by knocking down their fenced enclosure. By whatever means, the rabbits were liberated and from then on, Australia would never be the same.

THE RABBIT WAR

From Austin's estate, the bunnies hopped in all directions. About this time, farmers, sportsmen, and travelers were also introducing rabbits to many other parts of Australia. All of these rabbits bred rapidly and, with their gnawing front teeth, began stripping the continent of vegetation.

By 1880, two million acres of Victoria were officially proclaimed useless for farming and cattle grazing because of rabbit damage. The rabbits continued to spread—to northern New South Wales, southern Queensland, and even Western Australia. Rabbiting, or hunting rabbits, became a major Australian growth industry as professional rabbiters enthusiastically clubbed, trapped, shot, and poisoned the animals. In the first eight months of 1887, rabbiters killed over ten million rabbits in New South Wales alone.

The rabbits fueled the growth of several other industries as well. Rabbit meat was canned and shipped to England. Hatmakers turned the fur into top-quality felt hats. The damage the furry creatures caused, however, cancelled out any benefits they provided. Land values plummeted in rabbit-infested regions, and many farmers and ranchers met financial ruin. The rabbits spread so quickly that landowners often did not even know disaster had struck until it was too late. In 1879 at one sheep station, ranchers released 12,000 sheep to graze for the spring and summer. When the shepherds went to round them up the

In 1910, workers deliver dead rabbits to a freezing works for processing.

following fall, only 670 were left alive. The others had starved to death after a wave of hungry bunnies had stripped the land of food.

Over the next 70 years, Australians continued to wage war on the rabbits. They built fences and set up special netting to keep rabbits out. They brought in cats, mongooses, and other predators to eat the rabbits. More than anything, they relied on poisons, especially strychnine.

Unfortunately, the real victims of these efforts were not the rabbits, but the Australian wildlife. Wombats, emus, and kangaroos were shot and poisoned because they damaged rabbit netting. While failing to control rabbit numbers, imported predators dined heavily on native Australian birds and other wildlife. Marsupial opossums, tiger cats, wallabies, and bandicoots also died in large numbers from eating poisoned food meant for the rabbits. One farmer, who worked for years to keep rabbits off of his 14,400-hectare (36,000-acre) property, later wrote:

For months we persisted and certainly killed many thousands (of rabbits) but we could never get them all. Nature saved sufficient virile stock to re-infest the whole area in a single season. The slaughter of bird life was so tragic that I hate to contemplate it now. Poisoning is the worst of all methods.[3]

As the farmer points out, the irony in the war on rabbits was that none of the costly control efforts dented rabbit populations. Even when rabbits were exterminated in one area, their population quickly rebounded. Despite millions of dollars invested in killing rabbits, nothing kept the animals in check.

ANGEL OF DEATH

Not until 1950, did any relief appear in Australia's rabbit wars. In that year, Australian scientists conducted field tests with a virus called *myxomatosis*. Myxomatosis killed rabbits. It had been known to exist for more than 30 years, but early tests had been disappointing and plans to use it were abandoned. The persistent efforts of a physician named Jean Macnamara, however, convinced government officials to give the disease another chance.

Results of the new tests were immediate and dramatic. By 1953, after only three years, myxomatosis

47

*A typical rabbit hunting camp in
New South Wales in 1920*

had killed most of the rabbits in Australia—close to 750 million of them. The disease did not penetrate everywhere. Rabbits in some hilly regions seemed to escape the virus, but in many other parts of Australia, the animals were completely wiped out.

Many areas that had not been farmed or grazed for decades suddenly sprouted to life. Crops grew again, and by the mid-1950s Australian wool production soared to 31 million kilograms (70 million pounds) per year. For Australians, myxomatosis was a miracle. Unfortunately, it was short-lived. By 1955, the rabbits began to develop resistance to the virus. By 1967, despite several introductions of myxomatosis, rabbits reached about one-fifth of their peak populations. During the 1980s and 1990s, the bunnies were again overrunning vast tracts of Australia, destroying farmland and plundering many of Australia's most fragile ecosystems.

RABBIT STEW, OR WHY DID IT HAPPEN?

No one thing made the rabbit successful in invading Australia. A combination of ingredients produced the devastating stew that still simmers over the southern continent. The rabbit, though, tells us a lot about what makes many invaders so successful.

First, take the rabbit itself. Rabbits have many things going for them as invaders. One of the most important is that they can reproduce very rapidly. This is an important trait of almost all successful invaders. Rapid reproduction helps an invader in at least two ways. First, it allows the invader to establish a bridgehead in a new place quickly, reducing the chances it will be wiped out before it can spread. Second, it allows the invader to outgrow or outcompete other species around it. Bearing up to six litters per year, the rabbit was able to overwhelm Australia's native animals. Predators killed many rabbits, but plenty more survived to reproduce. The large numbers of rabbits also monopolized food, water, and other resources, robbing native animals of their livelihoods and eliminating the rabbits' competition.

A second useful trait of the rabbit is that it is a *generalist*. It can survive in a wide variety of conditions and circumstances. In Australia, rabbits demonstrate their generalist traits in a number of ways. They can eat many different foods, from grass and leaves to tree bark and roots. Because they live in burrows and have protective fur, they can also tolerate a wide variety of climates and temperatures. The rabbit occupies every kind of Australian habitat, from fertile farm country to harsh deserts almost devoid of water.

Rapid reproduction and a generalist lifestyle are two qualities that many of the world's most successful exotic invaders share with the rabbit. Scientists have also identified a number of other traits that may help an invader become successful. Some of these are listed in the box below. Many things that help make

Qualities of Good Invaders

Common qualities that contribute to an invader's success include:

- Rapid reproduction
- Generalist tendencies: an ability to survive in a wide variety of circumstances and environments
- Good ability to disperse or spread from place to place
- For plants, an ability to quickly drink up water and nutrients from the soil
- Leaving behind predators, diseases, and other enemies when invading a new place
- Being able to adapt or mutate into new forms that can survive new or changing conditions
- For plants, successful growth following fires and other disturbances
- Intelligence
- Genetic factors (suspected but still poorly understood)

*Cutting down rain forests to create cow pastures opens
the way for many invading plants and animals.*

a successful invader are still poorly understood.
Very little, for instance, is known about the genetic
properties that lead to an invader's success. This is
only one of many areas where more scientific research
needs to be done. The traits of an exotic species,
however, aren't the only ingredients that cook up a
successful invasion.

THE INVASION SITE

A second reason the rabbit was able to invade Australia
was because the country had been extensively altered
or disturbed by human activities. As the last chapter
indicated, habitat disturbances create the conditions
that allow many invasions to be successful. Distur-

*By killing native insects and other small animals,
the spraying of pesticides often makes a place
friendlier for exotic species.*

bances come in a variety of forms. Some are obvious, such as when a piece of forest is bulldozed to create a cow pasture. Other disturbances are more subtle. They can include:

- The removal of predators from a site by hunting or trapping
- The use of pesticides that kill native species or poison soil and water
- Burning to create pastures or farmland
- Overgrazing by sheep, goats, and cattle

*Impatiens are one of the many exotic plants
that people have imported for landscaping.
These showy flowers have invaded many natural
habitats, even undisturbed rain forests.*

- Pollution leading to acid rain or greater amounts of nutrients in rivers

- Toxic or nuclear waste contamination

No matter what form they come in, disturbances are gold mines for exotic species. By destroying native species, disturbances often eliminate competition and create conditions that help an invader.

In Australia, people disturbed the natural environment in many ways. Large tracts of Australia's forests, for example, were logged or burned to create pastures and farms. This helped the rabbit. Rabbits in general do not do well in forests, and the destruction of Australian forests created many new homes for the bunnies to live.

Even more important than deforestation was the slaughter of Australia's native wildlife. One of the first things Europeans did in their new country was set about killing dingoes, eagles, and other predators. This allowed the rabbit to survive in much greater numbers. Removal of other native wildlife by poisoning, hunting, and trapping also gave the rabbit more food, water, and space to increase its population.

One final ingredient, however, still had to be in place before the rabbit could invade the southern continent.

TRANSPORTATION—THE NOT-SO-MISSING LINK

All successful invasions have one thing in common: transportation. Before people, natural barriers—such as oceans, deserts, and mountains—prevented most organisms from invading new habitats. Now, thanks to us, invaders have a wide variety of transportation options. They include everything from cows and goats to modern ships, planes, and trucks. Viruses and other parasites even find transportation in our own bodies.

Human transportation has influenced not only the ability of organisms to travel but also where they travel to. A large proportion of the world's successful invaders, including the rabbit, originally came from Europe. This is no accident. For centuries, European countries were the centers of world trade. Today, as trading patterns change, more and more invaders are showing up from Asia, Latin America, and other regions.

In the modern world, whether plants and animals get transported depends on two things. The first is the organism's abilities to grab on to transportation. Some animals easily adapt to human modes of transport. Chapter 2, for example, described plants and animals that have taken advantage of ship ballast, canals, and the fur of animals to expand their ranges. Even more important than an organism's ability to grab is a second factor—people's desire to transport the organism for their own gain.

The previous pages have already presented a number of examples of how imports lead to invasions. One way is for undesirable species to be accidentally imported with desirable ones. Contaminated shipments of crop seeds, for instance, allowed at least 28 serious weed species to reach America in the nineteenth century.

Animals imported as pets are also a major source of invasions. Many pets escape or are released into the environment by thoughtless owners who grow tired of caring for the animals. At least 27 species of exotic fish, for example, have escaped or been released from aquariums to become established in U.S. waterways (see chapter 4).

The rabbit, however, was neither an undesirable import nor an escapee. People wanted the rabbit Down Under, and they bent over backward to make it a part of the Australian landscape. The rabbit is a case in which people simply failed to consider the enormous consequences of their actions.

It is far from the only case. Private individuals and government agencies around the world still provide the "final link" to biological invaders by intentionally importing them and releasing them into the wild. The United States is no exception. As the next chapter explains, both intentional and accidental invaders cause problems in every corner of America.

A group of starlings survey their conquered territory from a California telephone pole.

The Starling—Shakespeare's Mistake

In 1890, a New Yorker named Eugene Schieffelin came up with an amusing idea. He thought it might be nice to have all the birds mentioned in the plays of William Shakespeare living in New York City. With this in mind, Schieffelin brought 80 harmless-looking birds called starlings from England and released them in New York's Central Park.

One hundred years later, starlings occupy just about every corner of North America, from New York to Alaska to northern Mexico. These shiny black, yellow-beaked birds have even been sighted in one of the harshest places on earth, Death Valley!

Some people admire starlings. Like mockingbirds, they can imitate many sounds. Starlings also eat several pests, including the clover weevil and the Japanese beetle. The birds, though, pack far more problems than solutions.

Starling flocks can each number half a million birds or more. A flock of starlings can swoop down on a farm and devour a year's worth of grapes, cherries, or other crops in a single day. In 1976, starlings destroyed more grapes than any other pest. Starlings also eat the feed of livestock and even destroy feed with their rain of droppings.

Starlings spread human parasites and disease, such as tapeworms, encephalitis, liver fluke, and food poisoning. Starling nests are also breeding grounds for histoplasmosis, a serious airborne disease that damages our lungs.

One of the worst qualities of starlings is their aggressiveness. Starlings are fierce fighters, and they nest almost anywhere, including in the nests of other birds. If a starling finds a good nest, it kicks out or kills the bird that made the nest. Then, it smashes the other bird's eggs and takes over the nest for itself. In the northeastern U.S., starlings are blamed for the disappearance of bluebirds, flickers, and other songbirds. In Virginia, starlings may be driving red-headed woodpeckers to extinction.

With all of the problems they have brought, starlings are called "the most unpopular bird in America." One positive thing can be said for starlings, however; they've done little to damage Shakespeare's reputation.

four

Endangered States

According to the OTA report *Harmful Non-Indigenous Species in the United States*, more than 4,500 exotic species have become established in the United States. At least 200 of them cause serious harm. The cost of biological invaders to the U.S. economy has been staggering. Between 1906 and 1991, just 79 invaders cost the United States an estimated $97 billion. This total includes crop losses, direct damage to buildings and other structures, and money spent controlling the invaders. What's more, this figure represents only a small percentage of species known to cause problems. The report left out more than 85 percent of harmful exotic species, including agricultural weeds and human diseases.

The cost of biological invasions, however, goes beyond dollars and cents. Exotic species not only affect our wallets, but our health, our environment, and our quality of life as well. Few parts of our country are immune, but a number of states have been hit especially hard. Three of the worst are California,

	species analyzed b (number)	cumulative loss estimates (millions of dollars, 1991)	species not analyzed a (number)
Plants	15	603	—
Terrestrial vertebrates	6	225	>39
Insects	43	92,658	>330
Fish	3	467	>30
Aquatic invertebrates	3	1,207	>35
Plant pathogens	5	867	>44
Other	4	917	—
Total	79	96,944	>478

a *Based on estimated numbers of known harmful species per category*
b *Excludes most agricultural weeds*

NOTES: *The estimates omit many harmful NIS for which data were unavailable. Figures for the species represented here generally cover only one year or a few years. Numerous accounting judgments were nessary to allow consistent comparison of the 96 different reports relied on; information was incomplete, inconsistent, or had other shortcomings for most of the 79 species.*

Florida, and Hawaii. These states share much in common. All have warm or mild climates hospitable to exotic species. All are major ports of entry into the United States from other parts of the world. Most importantly, each of the three states is extremely attractive to people. The human invasions of all three states have led to massive disturbances of natural ecosystems and cleared the way for a host of other invading organisms.

CALIFORNIA

California contains one of the richest collections of ecosystems in the world. Driving across the Golden State, one can find desert, temperate rain forest, oak woodland, grassland, sand dune, chaparral, mountain, and dozens of other natural communities. These ecosystems support an incredible diversity of plants and animals. Six thousand three hundred species of flowering plants are native to California—more than can be found in the entire northeastern United States. Joining these plants are at least 200 mammal species, 28,000 insects, 525 birds, 129 amphibians and reptiles, and 113 species of freshwater fish.

Because the state is surrounded by such geographical barriers as deserts, mountains, and the Pacific Ocean, some biologists view California as an "ecological island."[1] Many of the state's native species, including more than one-third of its flowering plants, are found nowhere else on earth. The same qualities that make California attractive to plants and animals—warm winters, plentiful sunshine, and a variety of landscapes—also attract human invaders.

More than 30 million people have settled in California, making it the most populous state in the

Coast redwood forests are one of the many unique ecosystems that provide homes for California's wealth of native species.

nation. Their presence has had a dramatic impact on the environment. People have converted most of the California's natural grasslands to farmland. They've logged and mined large tracts of forests and swallowed up millions of acres of coastal scrub with sprawling cities, such as Los Angeles and San Diego. Four to five million domestic sheep and cattle graze California's forests, grasslands, deserts, and chaparral. To provide water for livestock, humans, and agriculture, people have dammed or diverted almost every natural waterway in the state.

In California, people and the disturbances that they have caused have spelled one thing for exotic species: opportunity.

Biological invaders have arrived in California by almost every possible route, including ports, airports, and highways. In 1990 alone, twenty-six million vehicles passed through the state's border stations. From these vehicles, agricultural inspectors confiscated more than 104,000 parcels that presented a risk of carrying harmful exotic species.

Agriculture is both a cause and a victim of many of the invaders arriving in the state. Agriculture is a $20-billion-a-year industry in California. The state leads the nation in total agricultural output and in producing more than 75 crop and livestock commodities, from eggs and onions to lettuce and pomegranates.

Agriculture has helped biological invaders in many ways. Contaminated seeds have been the source of a variety of California's weed species. Seeds of yellow star thistle, for instance, may have arrived mixed in crop seed in 1860. The thistle now infests 3.2 million hectares (8 million acres) in California, 8 percent of the state's land area. Exotic insects and other pests have also piggybacked into the state on imported

*Star thistle has rendered more than 2.2 million hectares
(8 million acres) of California useless for human
activities. Its seeds may have been brought
into the state mixed in with crop seeds.*

plants, live fish and shrimp, livestock, and other agricultural products.

Not all invaders arrive in California by accident. Most of the state's important agricultural plants and animals are exotic species that have been purposely introduced. The majority of these "behave" and do not invade native ecosystems, but some do escape to cause problems. Wild burros have overgrazed sensitive desert areas, such as Death Valley National Park, and may have contributed to the decline of the state's native bighorn sheep. Feral horses, cattle, sheep, goats, and pigs have also damaged sensitive ecosystems by overgrazing and tearing up plants and soil.

People's interest in gardening, fishing, and hunting has also helped invaders. More than 300 different plants, including some of the state's worst pests, have escaped from gardens to invade native ecosystems. These include French broom, Andean pampas grass, and ice plant. More than one-third of the state's freshwater fish species have been purposely introduced for sport, including striped bass, brown trout, and sunfish. Reptiles, amphibians, mammals, and birds have also been released in large numbers.

Biological invaders have cost California billions of dollars. Between the years 1981 and 1987 a single agricultural pest—the Mediterranean fruit fly, or Medfly—cost the state $350 million in crop losses and control efforts. Scientists predict that in the future Medfly and more than 200 other exotic crop pests will cost agriculture as much as $3 billion each year.

Exotic species also threaten the state in other ways. Weeds, such as gorse and star thistle, have rendered huge portions of the state useless for farming, grazing, and recreation. Exotic trees—such as tamarisk, or salt cedar—infest stream and river beds, plants.

Eucalyptus trees have been widely planted in California. Besides displacing native plants, the trees have been implicated in a number of fires, including the deadly blaze that swept through Oakland in 1991.

This, in turn, threatens native birds and other wildlife that depend on the native plants and a steady water supply to survive.

Exotic animals also kill native species directly. Imported fish have preyed on a host of native fish and amphibians, such as the mountain yellow-legged frog and arroyo toad. The red fox, brought to California for its fur and for fox hunts, threatens the rare San Joaquin kit fox and at least a half-dozen endangered birds, including the California clapper rail and California least tern.

As if all this wasn't enough, biological invaders pose significant public health problems. Exotic eucalyptus trees from Australia have been widely planted in California. The trees are highly flammable and have contributed to a number of fires in the state. One of these blazes, the 1991 Oakland Hills fire, killed 25 people, injured 150, and consumed more than 3,000 buildings.

Exotic diseases also threaten Californians. The California Department of Health Services regularly tracks more than 70 infectious diseases that occur in the state. Most of these are caused by exotic species. Lyme disease, for instance, is caused by an exotic bacterium. The disease, spread by biting ticks, entered California in 1978. Lyme disease can cause severe heart and nervous system disorders as well as permanent arthritis. Between 1990 and 1995, more than 1,100 cases of the disease were reported to the state's Department of Health Services.

Yet another type of public health risk, African, or killer, bees have invaded California from Mexico. These bees cause about 40 deaths a year in Latin America and are also expected to pose a threat to people living in California and other states.

A single African, or killer, bee is no more dangerous to a person than the more common European bee. African bees, however, often attack together to defend their nesting sites.

How Bad are Killer Bees?

In the United States, no biological invader has received more attention than the African honey bee, also known as the Africanized, or killer, bee. African bees began their invasion in 1956 when they escaped from a research laboratory in Brazil. From Brazil, they swarmed in all directions, expanding their range as much as 480 kilometers (300 miles) per year. Despite intensive efforts to stop them, the bees crossed into the state of Texas in 1990. By June, 1995, at least eight swarms had reached California.

African bees earned their nasty reputation from their aggressive defense of their hives. Unlike other bees, when African bees sense a threat they attack en masse. Hundreds, even thousands, of bees pursue enemies. At the same time, the African bee's danger to humans is often exaggerated. The sting of an individual bee is no worse than that of a common European honey bee. In Latin America, it is estimated that African bees kill about 40 people each year—about the same number who die of allergic reactions to bee stings in the United States.

Scientists believe that the biggest danger from African bees is not their threat to people but to the European honey bees that are already here. European honey bees are one example of an exotic species that has been useful to people. The bees were first introduced to the United States in 1621 and quickly became essential to pollinating the hundreds of crops grown here. Their value to U.S. agriculture is estimated to be about $20 billion per year—$4 billion in California alone. Many European bee colonies perform their pollination services without human supervision, but most are brought to farms by professional beekeepers.

Unfortunately, wherever the more aggressive African bees spread they kill European bees. African bees can pollinate crops like their European cousins, but they are much more difficult for beekeepers to manage. Some beekeepers in Brazil and elsewhere have learned to handle the African bees, but in most places African bees drive beekeepers out of business.

No one is quite sure how far the African bee will spread into the United States. Most people predict it will be able to survive only in warmer southern states, though others think it may do well all the way into Canada. Scientists are studying how to reduce the harmful effects of the bees and turn them into productive pollinators. So far, few breakthroughs have been made. Meanwhile, farmers, beekeepers, and anyone else living in African bee territory will have to watch their step and learn to get along with their touchy new neighbors.

FLORIDA

Florida is not called the Sunshine State by accident. As in California, the state's warm semi-tropical climate provides homes for a large variety of plants, animals, and people. Florida's economy, like California's, is closely tied to agriculture. Orange trees, sugar cane, cattle, and nursery and aquarium plants all contribute heavily to the state's economy. Florida is also a major destination for people and products from the Caribbean, Latin America, and around the world.

Florida does differ from California in some important respects, however. While California stays fairly dry, Florida is known for being wet. The state averages 1,346 millimeters (53 inches) of rain a year. Most of the land sits near sea level, so swamps and other wetland areas abound. People have worked hard to drain Florida's wetland areas and replace them with cities and farms. These massive disturbances, combined with Florida's location and climate, have created superb conditions for alien species.

More than 140 species of exotic birds have been spotted in Florida, including 11 that have become permanently established or *naturalized*. Florida is also home to 27 species of exotic reptiles and amphibians, more than any other state. More than one-quarter of Florida's 3,500 plant species are established invaders. So are 19 of the state's 80 freshwater fish and 40 of its 140 land snails.

The sources of these introduced organisms vary. Ornamental plants have spread into natural areas from people's gardens. Such pests as fire ants have been accidentally imported into the state with agricultural products (see chapter 5). Exotic birds, reptiles, mammals and fish have escaped as pets or been liberated by such natural disasters as Hurricane Andrew, which blasted across south Florida in 1992.

Although all of Florida's ecosystems have been affected by exotic species, Florida's waterways and wetland areas have perhaps been hardest hit. Exotic water weeds have choked many of Florida's canals, lakes, and rivers. The state's unique wetland areas, especially the Everglades, have suffered even more.

The Everglades covers about 10,360 square kilometers (about 4,000 square miles) of south Florida and is home to countless species of wildlife, including eagles, alligators, and the endangered Florida panther. Appreciated today for its value to wildlife and water quality, the Everglades and other wetlands were viewed as nuisances in the early part of this century. Developers, farmers, and civil engineers laid siege to these fragile wetlands by digging ditches, rerouting rivers, and planting exotic vegetation. One of their weapons was the paper bark tree, or melaleuca.

Originally from Australia, melaleuca is a fast-growing tree that sucks up water. Agricultural interests began planting the tree in the early 1900s with the goal of soaking up the Everglades and establishing useful forests in the area. Their plan backfired. The tree turned out to be nearly useless for lumber and has ended up rampaging across the state.

Miami International Airport is a major gateway for exotic plants and animals that are intentionally brought into the United States.

*Water hyacinth has invaded many waterways in south Florida,
including this canal in Big Cypress National Reserve.*

Florida's Terrible Trio

Water hyacinth has plagued Florida since it was introduced from South America in the 1880s. Cattlemen brought the plant to Florida, thinking it would provide good feed for their cattle. Although cattle never developed a fondness for water hyacinth, the plant did develop a fondness for Florida. Water hyacinth reaches densities of more than 1,600,000 plants per hectare (640,000 per acre) and can double its biomass in less than a week. By the 1950s, thick mats of water hyacinth clogged more than 48,000 hectares (120,000 acres) of Florida's waterways. The plant not only makes navigation impossible but also drastically reduces water quality and robs native water birds and other wildlife of valuable habitat.

Two other water weeds, waterlettuce and hydrilla, have also been purposely introduced to Florida and have spread to become pests. Through intensive and costly control efforts, water hyacinth and waterlettuce have been brought under control. This is not true of hydrilla. Hydrilla forms dense mats near the surface of the water. It blocks sunlight for other plants and harms fish by lowering the amount of oxygen in the water. In 1993, Florida spent approximately 5.5 million dollars to control hydrilla. Unfortunately, this is less than half the money needed to keep the plant in check. In recent years, hydrilla infestation has doubled from 20,000 to 40,000 hectares (100,000 acres) of Florida waterways. Without more money to combat the weed, it will continue to smother the state's lakes, canals, and rivers.

The flowers from a single melaleuca tree can produce millions of tiny seeds, which help to spread the tree.

Melaleuca's success sprouts from several sources. It reproduces rapidly, a single tree producing millions of tiny seeds each year. The tree also tolerates a wide range of soil conditions and can survive flooding, drought, and fire. Human disturbance of the Everglades probably also has helped. By channeling water away from the Everglades, people probably weakened or caused stress to native plants, which reduced their ability to compete with melaleuca. Like many successful invaders, melaleuca was also transported without

Melaleuca, or paper bark tree, has gobbled up enormous tracts of south Florida and has even invaded suburbs like this one in Miami.

its natural enemies. In Australia, more than 400 species of insects are known to attack melaleuca. Not so in Florida, where very few insects take on the tree.

With all of these advantages, melaleuca now infests more than 200,000 hectares (half a million acres) of the Everglades. Its spread has been devastating to native plants and animals. A pristine wetland area may contain between 60 and 80 species of native

Alligators are one of the countless species that are losing their homes to invading trees and water plants in the Florida Everglades.

plants. After melaleuca moves in, the total drops to three or four. Native birds and other wildlife also find little food in stands of paper bark. One Florida scientist referred to melaleuca forests as "biologically dead" compared to native wetlands and forests.[2]

Efforts to head off melaleuca and other invading trees in the Everglades have been expensive and so far ineffective. In one conservation area alone, it was estimated that the total cost of eradication would be $12.9 million over five years. For the whole state, eradication could easily cost hundreds of millions, if not billions, of dollars. Such funding has been hard to come by, however, and meanwhile melaleuca continues to gallop across south Florida at a rate of 20 hectares (50 acres) per day.

HAWAII

In many ways, Hawaii's history is similar to New Zealand's. The Hawaiian islands have been isolated since they were formed 70 million years ago. During that time, more than 10,000 species of Hawaiian plants and animals have evolved that are found nowhere else in the world. What makes these species so interesting is that, as in New Zealand, they originated from a small number of immigrants.

Forty species of colorful Hawaiian birds, called honeycreepers, evolved from one kind of finch that reached the islands from North or South America. More than one-quarter of the world's fruit flies, 600 species, evolved in Hawaii from a single insect ancestor. These examples and others give Hawaii more biodiversity per square kilometer (0.3 square mile) than anywhere else in the United States. They also make the islands a priceless living laboratory for biologists studying evolution.

Hawaiian honeycreepers have been devastated
by exotic predators, the destruction of forests,
and avian (bird) diseases.

Tragically, Hawaii has earned the reputation as the extinction capital of the United States. While making up only 0.2 percent of our nation's land area, the state has suffered almost three-quarters of our bird and plant extinctions. Seventy of Hawaii's 140 birds have gone extinct along with 10 percent of the state's plants. Most of Hawaii's remaining plant and animal species are also in danger.

The reasons for this tragedy should by now be familiar. As in New Zealand, human invaders have severely altered the state's natural ecosystems, especially in the lowlands. Almost all forest lands below 600 meters (2,000 feet) in elevation have been destroyed by agriculture and other human activities. An even greater danger has come from biological invaders brought by people.

Why are biological invaders such a problem in Hawaii? As in New Zealand a big reason is because many native species evolved without defenses against predators. More than one thousand species of native Hawaiian snails, for example, used to live in Hawaii's forests. In 1955, however, an exotic predatory snail called the rosy snail was introduced to control populations of another exotic snail called the African giant snail. The rosy snail hunted some giant snails, but it concentrated on Hawaii's native snails. As a result, as many as half of native snail species are now extinct.

Many native plants also evolved without protection from grazing animals. Grazing animals were absent from Hawaii until Europeans brought them in the eighteenth century. In areas where cows and goats are allowed to forage, they have virtually eliminated the defenseless native plants. On the other hand, grazing has helped hardier exotic plants, such as firetree and strawberry guava.

The danger of biological invaders, however, goes beyond the threat to plants and animals. It threatens Hawaiians themselves. Hawaii was one of the few places in the world without native mosquitoes. Since the 1800s, however, several mosquito species have been introduced. Two diseases that are spread by mosquitoes, avian malaria and avian pox, have already devastated Hawaiian birds. If new mosquito species

In many parts of Hawaii, natural forests have been replaced by strawberry guava trees.

become established, human diseases, such as malaria, may not be far behind.

Biological invaders may also threaten the state's watersheds. Miconia, for example, is a tree that devours rain forests. The tree has already taken over large parts of Tahiti and is now spreading through the Hawaiian islands of Maui and Oahu. Miconia not only robs native species of their homes but increases soil erosion. This, in turn, threatens water supplies by silting up dams and rivers.

One final threat to Hawaii is one that people often don't think about: the state's tourist industry. Tourism is Hawaii's biggest source of revenue and accounts for

Although it looks harmless, miconia has taken over many of Tahiti's native forests. Government and private officials are fighting to prevent a similar takeover in Hawaii.

more jobs than any other industry. In 1991, the state brought in $9.9 billion from almost seven million visitors. Most visitors come to enjoy and appreciate Hawaii's natural beauty, including its native species. Exotic species, however, can have a huge impact on tourists' perceptions of the islands. Mosquitoes, killer bees, biting flies and ants, and diseases could eventually transform Hawaii from a tourist paradise to just another bug-infested tropical backwater. Additional threats, such as the brown tree snake, could keep tourists away for good.

Scott Johnson works for the U.S. Fish and Wildlife Service trying to protect Hawaii's endangered species.

Exotic insects and the diseases that they carry could drive away tourists, such as this surfer, and the $9.9 billion they bring to the islands each year.

He and many other biologists see a vital connection between tourism and protecting Hawaii's native flora and fauna. "A lot of what we're trying to preserve is what brings tourists here," Johnson explains. "The exact same kind of stuff. Most tourists don't go to see a native honeycreeper, of course, but it's the idea that there *are* natural forests here. Or that people can fly over and see this beautiful scenery and say 'Geez, look at that beautiful place. We really want to save this.'"[3]

The question for Hawaii, Florida, and other endangered places is: Can the invaders be stopped?

The Brown Tree Snake versus The Dog Patrol

On December 20, 1994, workers at Hawaii's Schofield military base caught a snake. The snake was only about 50 centimeters (20 inches) long, but it sent shockwaves through Hawaii. The reason? The snake was a brown tree snake, an animal that had caused an ecological catastrophe on the island of Guam.

Originally from northern Australia, Papua-New Guinea, and the Solomon Islands, the brown tree snake probably hitchhiked to Guam aboard military equipment after World War II. By the 1980s, as many as 5,000 brown tree snakes crawled through every square kilometer of Guam's forest (13,000 snakes per square mile). The snakes bit people, shorted out power lines, and devastated Guam's wildlife. All ten of Guam's native forest birds disappeared. One of these, the Guam flycatcher, is now extinct. Two others, the Guam rail and the Micronesian kingfisher, survive only in captivity.

Government agencies are working aggressively to make sure the snake doesn't repeat its terrifying performance in the Aloha State. Some of their most effective weapons? Dogs.

Dogs' keen sense of smell and high intelligence make them ideal inspectors. On Guam, teams of dogs and handlers working for the U.S. government sniff out brown tree snakes from baggage and cargo leaving the island. The dogs are Jack Russell terriers and are trained to kill brown tree snakes on sight.

Dog teams also help keep brown tree snakes and other exotic species from entering Hawaii. In Hawaii, the state Department of Agriculture trains beagles to inspect incoming cargo and baggage from airline passengers. Beagles

were chosen over terriers because beagles are friendly-looking and have a nice personality that does not threaten tourists and other people the dogs must work around. In addition to searching for tree snakes, the dog teams also sniff out fruit, flowers, soil, and anything else that might be concealing pests. Over the years, the dogs have discovered turtles, Tokay geckos, parasitic worms, tropical fish, and a number of other exotic species. Their nose for nuisances makes the dogs valuable allies in Hawaii's efforts to keep exotic species out of the state.

Beagles (left) and Jack Russell terriers are some of the important weapons in keeping the brown tree snake (above) out of Hawaii.

five

Stopping Invaders—
and Leaving Them Alone

The previous chapters are filled with examples of exotic species and the damage they can do. As the species most responsible for the spread of invaders, people are also responsible for changing this destructive pattern. The question is: can biological invasions be stopped and, if so, how?

Biologists recognize three stages at which invaders can be dealt with. They can be stopped before or while they are trying to travel abroad; they can be eradicated once they arrive in a new country or place; or they can be controlled after they have invaded and become a problem.

KEEPING INVADERS OUT

Of the three methods for dealing with invaders, the first—prevention—is by far the easiest and cheapest. Prevention is carried out in two ways. One is by *inspection*, which has been used by government agencies around the world to prevent exotic species from entering new places.

*Border inspection stations help keep exotic plants
and animals from being introduced into new areas.
Unfortunately, many stations have been closed
by government budget-cutters.*

One well-known pathway for invaders to reach
new places is in the baggage of international travelers.
To keep this from happening, inspectors at airports,
border stations, and shipping ports examine baggage
by hand and with the help of X-ray machines and
other tools. Because of the huge volume of baggage
coming in, inspectors usually can't check every bag.
By identifying travelers from countries with known
pests, however, they can target people and bags that
pose the greatest risks.

Quarantine is a second method for preventing the
entry of exotic species. Quarantine is the process of
isolating and sometimes treating possible carriers of

pests and disease to make sure they are safe to bring into an area. Australia, New Zealand, the United States, and many other countries have extensive quarantines to prevent the entry of pests.

Quarantine methods vary depending on the types of trade goods and the types of stowaways they may carry. Quarantines are most often set up for live animals, agricultural goods, and other plant and animal products. Hawaii, for instance, has a quarantine of domestic pets to prevent rabies being introduced to the islands. Any dog or cat arriving in the state is kept in isolation for 120 days and is inspected to make sure the animal is not infected. Fresh produce, cut flowers, and other plant materials are also isolated and often treated with pesticides before being allowed into the state.

The effectiveness of inspection and quarantine depends both on having the technologies to stop pests and knowing when to use those technologies. Both of these factors require understanding the biology and behavior of exotic organisms. Unfortunately, the large number of potential invaders and lack of funds for research and inspection allows many exotics to get through.

In 1990, the USDA's Animal and Plant Health Inspection Service (APHIS) tried to evaluate the effectiveness of its inspection programs at Los Angeles International Airport. With the help of California state agencies, inspectors checked every piece of baggage from 153 targeted flights—those with high probabilities of carrying pests. They also inspected several random, non-targeted flights. Altogether, 16,997 passengers and their bags were checked. On targeted flights, inspectors discovered 667 lots of prohibited fruits and vegetables and 140 animal products. On non-targeted flights, they found 690 lots and 185 animal

EXAMPLES OF TREATMENT TECHNOLOGIES FOR IMPORTING COMMODITIES

Chemical treatment:

Commodities are treated with chemical fumigants at specific atmospheric pressures for specific time periods.

Example: Under normal atmospheric pressure and at 90–96°F, imported chestnuts are fumigated for 3 hours with methyl bromide for infestations of the chestnut weevil (*Curculio elephas*).

Temperature treatment:

Freezing:

Fruits and vegetables are frozen at subzero temperatures with subsequent storage and transportation handling at temperatures no higher than 20°F.

Cold treatment:

Commodities are cooled and refrigerated for specific temperatures and days.

Example: Fruit infested with the false codling moth (*Crytophlebia leucotreta*) requires refrigeration for not less than 22 days at or below 31°F.

Vapor heat:

Commodities are heated in water-saturated air at 110°F. Condensing moisture gives off latent heat, killing eggs and larvae.

Example: The temperature of grapefruit from Mexico is raised to 110°F at the center of the fruit in 8 hours and is held at that temperature for 6 hours.

Hot water dip:

Commodities are treated with heated water for specific periods of time.

Example: Mangoes weighing up to 375 grams from Costa Rica are dipped in 115°F water for 65 minutes.

Combination treatment:

Combination of fumigation and cold treatment.

Example: Fruit infested with Mediterranean fruit fly (*Ceratitis capitata*) is exposed to methyl bromide for 2 hours then refrigerated for 4 days at 33–37°F.

Irridation treatments:

Commodities are exposed to irridation at specific rates and times.

Example: Papayas shipped from Hawaii would be treated with a minimum absorbed ionizing radiation dose of 15 kilorads. (This treatment schedule has USDA approval but is not commercially used at this time.)

products. This blitz exercise demonstrated that many illegal shipments slip through current inspection programs and that more money and inspectors are needed to stem the flow.

Education is one weapon against the tide of illegal goods. Using posters, advertisements, and fliers, the USDA and other agencies try to warn travelers about transporting high-risk fruits, animals, and other products. These programs have mixed results. In Hawaii, government agencies and conservation groups have urged commercial airlines to show travelers a short video that explains the dangers of introduced pests. At the time this book was being written, however, at least two major U.S. airlines, Northwest and United, were refusing to show the video. These airlines have made it clear that protecting Hawaii's natural resources is not a priority for them. The result is that many travelers continue to be unaware of the dangers of transporting fruits, vegetables, and other high-risk commodities.

LEGAL LOOPHOLES AND OTHER STUMBLING BLOCKS

Unfortunately, even if inspections, quarantines, and education worked perfectly to stop prohibited exotic species, many more exotic organisms would continue to invade our shores. One reason is that inspections and quarantines fail to cover a variety of imports and circumstances. Regulations to prevent invasions from ballast water, for example, have been set up for the Great Lakes but not for other U.S. ports. Programs to inspect first-class mail between Hawaii and California fail to cover mail between Puerto Rico and California.

An even stickier problem is the shortage of laws designed to stop exotic species. In the United States,

Educational posters help warn airplane travelers of the dangers of carrying agricultural products to new places.

the vast majority of plants and animals from around the world can be legally imported with few or no restrictions. Prevention efforts focus on species that could damage crops or affect public health, but they ignore other categories of imports. Most fish and wildlife imports, for instance, are permitted to enter our country until they are proven to cause harm. Almost all of the world's plants can also be legally imported without restrictions.

Poor communication and cooperation between government agencies adds to the problem. A plant or animal that is recognized as a pest by one agency may be totally ignored by another. For instance, at least nine species of harmful weeds that are illegal to import into the United States may be legally transported between states once they are here.

Also, many agencies that could help monitor or control biological invaders do not have enough money or employees to do so. The U.S. Fish and Wildlife Service, for example, has the legal authority to prevent many wildlife products from entering the United States, but has a budget of only $3 million per year— enough to inspect only a fraction of the shipments coming into the country. On the other hand, the USDA's Animal and Plant Health Inspection Service receives at least $100 million annually for its agricultural inspection and pest-control efforts.

Some government agencies, businesses, and conservation groups are beginning to work together to overcome problems of communication and funding. In Hawaii, a group of more than 80 professionals representing public and private interests have created an Alien Species Action Plan. The plan focuses on strengthening Hawaii's defenses against biological invaders. One of the group's first actions was to improve inspection of first-class mail into the state, a source of 20 percent of Hawaii's insect pests that arrive each year. The group hopes to accomplish even more in the future. Hawaii's efforts set an important example for how other groups and agencies can work together to slow down the spread of exotic species.

THE SECOND LINE OF DEFENSE—ERADICATION

Because of the gaps in stopping exotic species from entering new places, many invaders become firmly established before anyone realizes they're there. In these cases, one may ask, "Why don't we just get rid them?"

This solution seems simple, but is not always possible or desirable. As chapter 3 explained, not all invaders actually do us great harm. The report *Harmful Non-Indigenous Species* in the United States estimated that only between 4 and 19 percent of aliens cause significant problems in our country, while most other invaders keep a low profile and actually go unnoticed much of the time. Other invaders, such as honey bees from Europe, actually bring us benefits. Clearly, trying to get rid of these useful and low-impact exotics is not in our best interest. But what about the problem species?

In certain situations, getting rid of a species, or *eradicating* it, is the answer. One of these situations is when an invader is discovered early. Early detection of the Asian tiger mosquito, for instance, allowed authorities to wipe out the insect quickly in Minnesota, California, and New Mexico. In Florida, on the other hand, the mosquito was not noticed until it had become well-established. By then, it proved impossible to get rid of.

A second case in which eradication is desirable is when an invader is limited to a small range or population. Small islands are excellent candidates for eradication efforts. Islands have the advantage of being limited in size. They can be quickly surveyed and often contain unique native species that are especially worth protecting. These factors have made them the targets of a number of successful eradication programs. New Zealand has successfully eradicated rats

*Animal control expert Homer Leong (top) sets a live trap
to protect one of Hawaii's wildlife refuges from
wild cats (bottom), mongooses, and rats.*

from several small islands by dropping poisoned baits for the rats to eat. Once they are cleared of rats, the islands are used to provide homes for endangered birds and other species. Similar successes have been achieved eradicating sheep and other pests from California's Channel Islands National Park.

A third situation in which eradication may be the best solution is when an invader is extremely harmful. A number of human diseases fall into this category. Malaria kills more than two million people each year and is considered the world's greatest threat to public health. The disease was originally restricted to Europe, Africa, and other parts of the Old World, but it has been accidentally carried to many other parts of the planet by people. Because it is so destructive, however, the disease has been at least temporarily eliminated from parts of Brazil, the United States, and other countries through expensive efforts to control mosquitoes that carry the disease.

A second Old World disease, smallpox, has been the target of an even more ambitious eradication effort. In 1966, the World Health Organization (WHO) began an all-out campaign to eradicate smallpox, a disease that was killing as many as two million people each year. Millions of people were vaccinated against the disease, and by May 1980 WHO officials declared that smallpox had been totally eliminated worldwide. In the cases of both malaria and smallpox, the harm the diseases caused outweighed the enormous expense and effort of eradicating them.

Although eliminating diseases and other harmful biological invaders is sometimes possible, in most cases it is not. The high cost of totally eradicating exotic species could quickly overwhelm national budgets around the world. Also, once an exotic species has become well-established, it is simply impossible

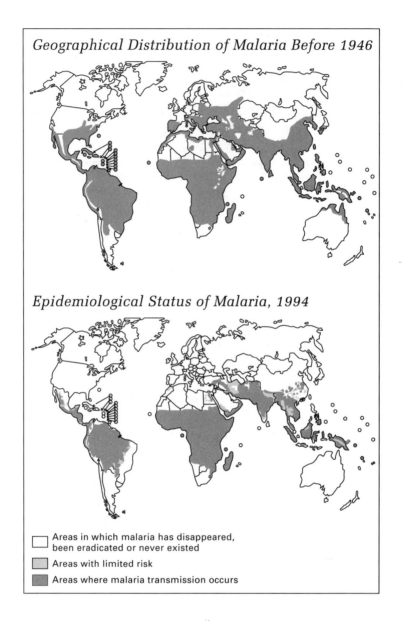

Geographical Distribution of Malaria Before 1946

Epidemiological Status of Malaria, 1994

☐ Areas in which malaria has disappeared,
been eradicated or never existed

▨ Areas with limited risk

▓ Areas where malaria transmission occurs

to get rid of in most cases. For instance, even though malaria has been eliminated from some places, it has proved impossible to eradicate from many countries where it is firmly established. The fire ant is a second example of an established invader that has foiled our best efforts to outsmart it. For malaria, the fire ant, and most other problem invaders, the name of the game is not eradication, but control.

The Red Menace

Fire ants receive their name from the intense burning sensation caused by their stings. Originally from South America, fire ants were first sighted in the United States in Mobile, Alabama, in 1929. The ants probably arrived on rocks and soil that were used as ship's ballast. Hitching rides with nursery plants, the tiny red or black insects quickly spread. By 1953, they had been found in 102 counties in ten southern states. It wasn't long before they were stinging people, damaging crops, and interfering with farm equipment throughout the South.

Congress officially declared war on the fire ant in 1957. The goal: to totally eradicate "the red menace." From 1961 through the mid-1970s, the pesticide Mirex was sprayed over 56 million hectares (139 million acres) of the South in an effort to exterminate the fire ant. The cost to taxpayers exceeded $172 million.

Unfortunately, Mirex harmed wildlife more than it hurt the fire ant. Worse still, the eradication program actually helped the fire ant become established by wiping out native insects that competed with the ants. Ant expert E.O. Wilson goes so far as to refer to the fire-ant program as "the Vietnam of entomology—and about as successful."[1]

Fire ants (top) attack and kill many native insect species,
such as this caterpillar (bottom).

The fire-ant program's failure, however, offers a number of valuable lessons about exotic species. First, keeping an invader out of a place is much easier and cheaper than getting rid of it once it has become established. Second, before we declare war on an exotic species, we need to understand our "enemy's" biology and behavior. Finally, facts are better guides than emotions when dealing with exotic species. The economic costs of fire ants, for example, have never been as bad as people think. The ants have harmed crops and damaged roads by digging under them. They also sting millions of people each year. On the other hand, the ants have done some good by helping to control such pests as the cotton boll weevil.

Biologists have stepped up efforts to learn about the fire ant and look for a solution to the fire-ant problem. Until a cure is found, however, the fire-ant experience demonstrates how in some exotic species battles, an uneasy truce is a better strategy than total victory.

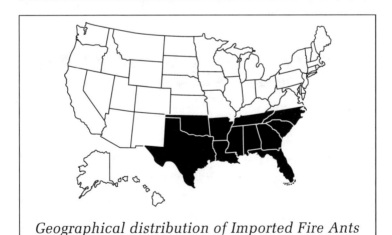

Geographical distribution of Imported Fire Ants

MODERN MANAGEMENT AND BIOLOGICAL CONTROL

People can control biological invaders in a number of ways. Exotic animals can be shot, trapped, poisoned, and kept out by fencing or other means. Exotic plants can be pulled, cut, plowed under, sprayed, and burned. Exotic diseases can be battled with antibiotics, vaccines, quarantines, and health education.

No control methods, however, are problem-free, and most are extremely expensive. In Florida, state and federal agencies have spent $120 million controlling exotic water plants between 1980 and 1992. In Hawaii, fences erected to keep pigs and goats out of Haleakala National park cost $2.4 million to construct and approximately $130,000 each year to maintain. On a national level, the United States spends approximately $7.4 billion on pesticides each year, mostly to control exotic agricultural pests and other biological invaders that cause economic damage.

Control of animal invaders—especially by trapping, poisoning, and hunting—has also raised concern from animal rights groups about cruelty to animals.

Biological Invasions and Animal Rights

Both private conservation groups and government agencies that are trying to control exotic species sometimes face criticism from animal rights groups. Several years ago, a group called PeTA (People for the Ethical Treatment of Animals) criticized The Nature Conservancy in Hawaii for using snares to kill feral pigs and other hoofed animals that were damaging

Many plants, such as this exotic cactus surrounding the water tower, have to be cleared by hand and hauled away.

native rain forests. PeTA argued that The Nature Conservancy, a private conservation organization, and other groups should use more humane methods to deal with the exotic animals, or that the exotic species should simply be left alone.

Although it's true that controlling biological invaders often involves killing them, it's also true that The Nature Conservancy and other groups spend a great deal of time and money searching for the most humane methods of dealing with exotic species. A real problem for conservation groups and government agencies, however, is the shortage of money available for animal control. Limited budgets often mean that difficult choices have to be made. In some cases, the most humane and effective method to remove exotic animals is by erecting fences to keep them out of an area. Exotic animals that are left inside the enclosed areas are then shot by professional hunters. In other cases, live-trapping is the best method. In remote forest areas, though, snares are the only method that is both effective and affordable.

The Nature Conservancy's Alan Holt explains, "When you have a conflict between an introduced organism and a native organism or ecosystem, it's tough. We tend to cast these invaders as enemies and evil, but these aren't bad plants or bad animals, and I think very few of us involved with managing ecosystems hate these organisms. The way we control them needs to be as humane and as respectful as possible, both of the exotic species themselves and of the planet."

At the same time, Holt argues that it's not ethical to focus on the suffering of an exotic species without considering the suffering that the exotic species is causing to native species.

An example of this suffering involves avian malaria. Avian malaria is an exotic disease that is spread by exotic mosquitoes in Hawaii. The mosquitoes are common in some parts of Hawaii because of exotic pigs. The pigs dig holes, or wallows, in the soil, and the wallows fill up with water and make ideal breeding sites for the mosquitoes. When the mosquitoes bite native birds and infect them with avian malaria, however, the birds undergo excruciating deaths.

Open sores break out all over their bodies, and then the birds' beaks and toes rot off. By getting rid of the pigs, conservation workers reduce the number of mosquitoes that are breeding. In doing so, they reduce the suffering of native birds and prevent honeycreepers and other endangered birds from going extinct.

In an article in *The Vegetarian Times*, Alan Holt explained The Nature Conservancy's position and found that most of the magazine's readers, including PeTA members, supported the Conservancy.

"Most people assumed that PeTA's description of us was correct," Holt explains. "They assumed that we were uncaring, ill-informed, callous, motivated by money, and lazy. We at least convinced people that we are not those things and that, in fact, we are facing a much broader set of issues and considerations than PeTA dared to tell them about. I think we showed that we've weighed those considerations very carefully and have adopted a position that is quite reasonable for most people."[2]

Perhaps the biggest difficulty with control methods, however, is that they usually have to be carried out year after year—forever. In an effort to overcome this difficulty, many people have looked to *biological control* for solutions.

Biological control, or biocontrol, is the practice of releasing predators or diseases that can control the populations of problem species. Chapter 3 described how the biocontrol agent myxomatosis was used to reduce rabbit populations in Australia. Other diseases are also being tested to control rabbits.

Australian Rabbit Update

As this book was going to press, a new weapon had been released in Australia's war on rabbits. Rabbit calicivirus, also known as rabbit haemorrhagic virus, is a virus that has killed hundreds of millions of rabbits in Asia and Europe since its appearance in 1984. On those continents, scientists have searched for a way to prevent the virus from killing rabbits in the wild and on rabbit farms. Australian and New Zealand scientists, however, recognized the virus as a potentially valuable biocontrol agent.

Tests were first conducted on the virus in early 1995 on Wardang Island off the coast of South Australia. By November, however, the virus had escaped into several populations of wild rabbits on the mainland. According to Dr. Brian Cooke, who leads the team of Australian and New Zealand scientists investigating the virus, results have been swift and dramatic.

"We've seen more than 95% mortality based on spotlight counts and confirmed by trapping," said Cooke in early December, 1995. "In one area that had been heavily infested, we trapped only one rabbit despite using 45 cage-traps. This area had over one hundred warrens (rabbit dens) per square kilometre."

"At Thackaringa Station, near Broken Hill," Cooke added. "Rabbit calicivirus was first reported about two weeks ago. About 80% of rabbits have died there. . . . Initially younger rabbits survive, but later, perhaps due to predator pressure, they are disappearing as well. The virus appears to be spreading to new areas up to 100 kilometers [sixty miles] apart and then infilling between these areas occurs."[4]

Cooke and his team will continue to monitor the spread of the virus. Meanwhile, the Australian goverment is leaning toward intentionally introducing the virus to other parts of the country. Public support for controlling the rabbits is overwhelming, and public officials hope that combining the virus with traditional rabbit control measures will finally allow them to get the upper hand on the rampaging rabbits.

Biocontrol has been used on other pests as well. In the 1890s, Australian ladybird beetles were brought to California to eat a kind of scale insect that was sucking the life from the state's orange trees. The beetles ended up saving California's citrus industry. In China, weaver ants have been used for more than 1,700 years to protect fruit trees from insect pests. The ants make nests out of the fruit trees' leaves. At the same time, they protect the trees by attacking and eating any other insects that come along. Weaver ants are the oldest known example of biocontrol on earth.

These dramatic examples have led many people to believe that biocontrol is the ultimate answer to our exotic species problems. This is not the case. Biocontrol has backfired in many situations. Chapter One described how stoats, ferrets, and weasels were brought to New Zealand to help control rabbit populations but preyed on native birds and other animals. The mongoose is another mammalian predator that was introduced to Hawaii and several Caribbean islands to control rat populations. Instead, it has wound up dining on native honeycreepers, shorebirds, and other native species.

Ladybird beetles have been an effective biological control agent in the war against some exotic insect pests.

In 1935 Australian sugarcane farmers unleashed a different kind of biocontrol disaster called the cane toad. The toad was originally from Latin America, and its mission in Australia was to eat two kinds of beetles that were devastating the country's sugar industry. Unfortunately, the toads ate almost everything *except* the beetles. This might not have been a problem, but the cane toad also reproduced rapidly and had poisonous skin glands that made it totally unpalatable to local predators. With these advantages, the toad ended up invading millions of acres of northeastern Australia. It has gobbled up countless smaller native animals and has poisoned many larger ones, including kookaburras, snakes, lizards, and endangered native cats. Scientists have found no way to stop the toad, and it is still spreading today—a constant reminder of the danger of introducing species outside their natural range.

Today, people are much more careful about which animals they release as biocontrol agents, but even so, biocontrol is usually no magic bullet for the exotic species problem. Patrick Conant is an entomologist working on biocontrol for Hawaii's Department of Agriculture. His department looks for insects, fungi, and other biocontrol agents that can slow the spread of exotic pests and other invaders. "The way I look at it," says Conant, "with biocontrol, you're rarely going to approach ninety percent control. If you can get insects that attack the seeds and flowers of an exotic plant, for example, you'll slow the plant down and maybe stop it from spreading, but it will still be out there."[3]

Biocontrol is not cheap, either. Because of earlier disasters with the mongoose and other species, biocontrol candidates are now run through a long and expensive series of tests before they are released into the environment. Before they can release a biocontrol

*The mongoose (top) and cane toad (right, top)
are two reasons why biocontrol agents are
now thoroughly tested in labs like this one
(right, bottom) before they are released.*

agent nowadays, scientists must prove that it can be effective and that the agent won't itself become a pest or attack native plants and animals. This evaluation process can take several years and cost hundreds of thousands of dollars. In Hawaii, for instance, only about three new biocontrol agents are released into the environment each year.

Because of biocontrol's shortcomings, farmers and natural resource managers must still depend on pesticides and other traditional control measures to keep from being overrun by exotic species.

Are the costs and effort worth it? A look at our exotic future may help answer that question.

six

Shaping Our Exotic Future

FACT: *Biological invaders are here to stay. As time goes on their numbers will increase and so will the problems they cause. What does this mean for our future? Even more important, what should we do about it?*

COSTS OF AN EXOTIC WORLD

As new species invade different parts of the world, they will continue to affect our economy, health, and environment. We can't predict every way in which this will happen. For example, we won't fully know the effects of genetically engineered organisms for decades to come. We also don't know how exotic species will take advantage of global warming and other environmental changes. We can predict many things, however.

More insect and fungus invasions are sure to lead to increased costs for farmers as they are forced to do battle with a larger number of pests. Farmers will pass

Engineering Life

A major concern for scientists and the public is the growing number of genetically engineered organisms on our planet. Genetically engineered organisms are also known as *GEOs* or *transgenic organisms*. They are species that have had genetic material or *genes* from other species inserted into them. A variety of techniques have been developed to insert the new genes. Scientists have discovered certain viruses and bacteria, for example, that can place genes from one organism into another one.

The kinds of genes inserted into GEOs vary. Genes to improve looks or flavor, or to allow an organism to resist pests, are commonly inserted into crop plants. Genes to increase growth rates and resistance to disease are added to fish and other animals.

The first GEO was released into the outdoors in 1986. Since then, hundreds of other transgenic species have been tested and some have even reached the marketplace. In December 1994, for instance, the USDA approved the sale of a transgenic yellow crookneck squash. It was the first approval of a crop plant engineered to resist viruses.

Biologists classify all GEOs as exotic or nonindigenous species because GEOs contain new sets of genes that are not found in any other organisms. GEOs cause all of the same concerns that other exotic species do, but they also raise a new set of special worries.

One major concern is whether GEOs will escape farms and other controlled conditions into the natural environment. If this happens, many scientists worry that the GEOs will combine or *hybridize* with weed species to form super weeds. With genes to resist pests, grow rapidly, and acquire nutrients and water, super weeds might devastate native species and defeat efforts to control them.

Hybridizing with native species might also allow GEOs to reduce biodiversity by changing or destroying native species. Newly developed strains of genetically engineered cotton, for example, might hybridize with native cotton plants in Hawaii. This will effectively destroy the native cotton species and rob us of genetic material that we may need in the future.

The USDA, Environmental Protection Agency (EPA), and Food and Drug Administration (FDA) all have guidelines for testing, producing, and marketing GEOs. So far, most GEOs have posed limited risks. But as research and technology develops, the variety and threat of GEOs are sure to increase. The Office of Technology Assessment and public interest groups, such as the Union of Concerned Scientists, believe that current guidelines fall short of what is needed to make sure that future GEOs will be safe. Almost none of the current regulations, for example, consider what might happen if GEOs invade natural areas, such as our national forests and parks. They also do not consider whether the behavior of GEOs might change in different countries or environments.

Another major drawback is that most current guidelines for GEOs are voluntary. A set of guidelines, for instance, has been established for researchers working with transgenic fish, but the guidelines do not include penalties for scientists who fail to follow the established recommendations.

"BOVINE GROWTH HORMONE MILK..... GENETICALLY ALTERED BAKED POTATO WITH MARGARINE.....
THE CRAZY FOOL WAS LIVING ON THE EDGE, CHIEF."

Public health concerns about GEOs are also increasing. In 1993, dairy farmers received approval to begin using a new genetically engineered drug called bovine growth hormone (BGH) to boost their cows' milk production. The FDA concluded that the milk from hormone-treated cows would not harm people, but BGH has been found to increase disease among the cows. This effect has raised concerns about whether the milk from these cows is really safe to drink. The Union of Concerned Scientists and public interest organizations have protested the use of BGH and called for stricter and more complete guidelines for all categories of GEOs.

113

these costs on to consumers, who will have to pay higher prices for food. People will also have to pay more to control pests in their own homes as exotic termites attack buildings and exotic insects, worms, and fungi infest trees and gardens.

New biological invasions will also undermine public health. Viral diseases, such as AIDS, will continue to spread through direct human contact. Mosquitoes and other exotic disease carriers will also spread. This will lead to a rising number of outbreaks of malaria, dengue fever, yellow fever, and other deadly ailments.

HIV and other Exotic Killer Viruses

In recent years, we have witnessed the spread of an alarming number of exotic diseases that foil the human body's attempts to defeat them. HIV, or human immunodeficiency virus, is a deadly killer that afflicts almost every country of the world. HIV causes the disease AIDS, acquired immunodeficiency syndrome. HIV eventually kills almost 100 percent of the people it infects. The virus can take years to kill, however, giving victims many opportunities to infect others.

HIV probably originated in Africa, where it may have been transmitted from monkeys to human beings. In people, the virus has most often been spread by sexual contact, used hypodermic needles, and blood transfusions of HIV-contaminated blood.

Young people are especially at risk from HIV, because they have sex more frequently and with more partners than other age groups. Abstaining from sex, staying with one partner, and faithfully using condoms reduce the risk of infection.

Millions of dollars are being spent in an attempt to find a cure for AIDS. Millions more are being spent educating people about its causes and how to keep from contracting the disease. Far more funds are needed. The U.S. State Department has estimated that forty-eight million people worldwide will be infected by HIV by the year 2000. Other estimates run much higher.

Unfortunately, HIV is not the last exotic killer virus we are likely to encounter. In 1995, an outbreak of ebola virus in Zaire, Africa killed approximately 80 percent of those infected—more than 200 people in all. HIV, ebola, and other viruses send an urgent warning to all nations to put greater effort and financial resources into scientific research, open communication, and public health education.

Biodiversity will pay one of the heaviest tolls to exotic organisms. Noted Harvard biologist E. O. Wilson estimates that already, more than 27,000 species of plants and animals are going extinct every year. As exotic species continue to spread, the rate of extinctions will rise. Especially at risk will be species that do not compete well with exotic organisms: plants and animals in such places as New Zealand and Hawaii.

Loss of biodiversity threatens us in many ways. More frequent floods, fires, and other natural disasters are already occuring as ecosystems lose species and become more unstable. Global extinctions also lead to the permanent loss of many plant and animal species that may have important uses in medicine and agriculture. So far, forty-seven major drugs, including those used to treat lukemia and malaria, have been discov-

Condoms are one of the most effective methods to prevent the spread of AIDS. Here, a billboard in Costa Rica urges people to use condoms when engaging in sexual activity.

ered in tropical plants alone. By allowing species to keep disappearing, we may be throwing away future cures for cancer, AIDS, and other diseases. We also may be destroying plants that could help feed our growing human population. These consequences give us enough reasons to be concerned about biological invasions. One final way that biological invasions affect us, however, is often overlooked: the way we view our planet.

WHAT IS NATURAL?

Already, most urban areas and many rural ones are overrun by exotic plants and animals. In a typical California suburb, you might see trees from Australia, shrubs from New Zealand, rats from Asia, and birds

*Many neighborhoods in California and elsewhere
have been landscaped almost exclusively with
exotic trees and other plants.*

from Europe. How do we know what is natural? The question is becoming harder and harder to answer.

When most of us think of the great American West, for example, a common image that pops into our heads is that of a tumbleweed rolling past a herd of cows being driven by cowboys on horseback. Yet none of these images was a part of the West when European explorers first traveled across North America. The tumbleweed originally came from Russia and quietly hitchhiked here with flax seeds. Cows and horses were imported intentionally from Europe. Even the cowboys or their ancestors came from Europe and other places to invade the new frontier.

Tumbleweeds are just one exotic species that has confused our ideas about what is natural.

Some argue that the replacement of native species by exotics is no big deal. For others, the loss of native plants and animals is nothing less than the loss of our culture and heritage. In Hawaii, native peoples are currently rediscovering their cultural past and identity. Native Hawaiian plants and animals play an important role in that process. Much of Hawaiian culture, for instance, centers around a native tree called a koa. The koa, though, has been heavily logged for making carvings and in most places has been replaced by exotic trees and other plants.

Biologist Art Medeiros was born in Hawaii and explains the significance of protecting the koa. "Koa in Hawaii is used as a kind of analogy for warrior," Medeiros says. "A strong person is called a 'koa'. It's the canoe-building wood and with it come all the native birds that depend on it. It's a tremendous cultural storehouse. As I tell some of my Hawaiian friends, if the Hawaiian forest goes down the drain, you might as well be living in San Jose, California, because it won't matter so much where you are, just as long as all the people are there."[1]

The koa is only one reminder of how much Hawaiians and the rest of us have to lose if our native plants and animals disappear.

SETTING THINGS RIGHT

There is no simple solution to the problem of biological invasions. Even if we put all our energy into stopping them, some species will continue to slip through our inspections, quarantines, and other defenses. People could do far more, however, to slow the spread of exotic species and limit the damage they cause. This is especially true for the large number of plants and animals that we deliberately take to new places.

In the United States, laws and regulations could be vastly improved to regulate exotic species. The OTA report *Harmful Non-Indigenous Species of the United States* states that our current government approach is "a largely uncoordinated patchwork of laws, regulations, policies, and programs"[2] that does not nearly match the problems we face.

Previous chapters have already described how most exotic species can be legally imported into the United States until they are proven to be a problem. Laws that restrict harmful weeds and wildlife do exist, but before a species can be legally kept out of the country, it must be placed on an official list, which is an arduous and time-consuming process.

Controlling exotic species is made more difficult by the fact that policies between different government agencies vary tremendously. The National Park Service has fairly strict policies to keep exotic species out of our national parks, monuments, and historical sites. On the other hand, the Natural Resources Conservation Service (formerly the Soil Conservation Service, or SCS) still actively promotes and releases some exotic species without thoroughly investigating whether they might cause problems.

The policies of individual states also range from loose to relatively strict. The OTA report listed several states that have made determined efforts to control exotics, including Florida, Georgia, Hawaii, Montana, and Utah. In contrast, Mississippi, North Dakota, Ohio, Texas, and West Virginia have put little energy into regulating invaders.

It is beyond the scope of this book to describe every law and policy that could be improved to control biological invasions. The preceding examples, however, suggest that what we need is a new way of looking at exotic species. Instead of allowing all species to come in until they are proven to be harmful, we should ask ourselves: are there clear benefits to bringing in *any* exotic plant or animal? If so, what are the dangers? Only after answering these two questions, should we even consider allowing a new species into the country.

This approach is gaining popularity. The National Park Service, the Bureau of Land Management, and a number of state agencies have begun to adopt stricter controls on exotic species. Conservation groups have also begun to work on guidelines that would reduce the rate of biological invasions around the world.

The International Union for the Conservation of Nature and Natural Resources (I.U.C.N.) has proposed a model national law that would include the following policies:

- allow release of an exotic species only if it would result in clear, well-defined benefits

- allow release of exotic species only if no suitable native species were available

- prohibit the release of exotic species into any natural areas and require that any planned releases undergo complete testing to make sure that they would not cause problems and could be controlled if necessary.

An example of what is possible can be seen in New Zealand. As chapter 1 described, New Zealand has suffered terribly from exotic species introductions. In recent times, though, the country has worked hard to protect itself from further invasions. New Zealand has placed a top priority on regulating exotic species and has passed a number of national policies to prevent accidental invasions and closely evaluate intentional releases.

People who work with exotic species consider New Zealand's approach a common-sense standard for other countries to shoot for. How soon such policies might be adopted in the United States, however, is uncertain. Nursery, pet, aquaculture, and agriculture industries usually oppose any regulations that might threaten their profits. The new Congress elected in 1994 also launched an all-out attack on many of our nation's existing environmental laws, including the Endangered Species Act, the Clean Water Act, the Clean Air Act, and the Safe Drinking Water Act. In this political atmosphere, the chances of Congress passing any new laws to protect the environment are highly unlikely.

OTHER STEPS FORWARD

Even without new laws and regulations, however, much can be done to stem the rate of biological invasions. As is often the case, many of these involve money. Chapter 5 described how funds are needed to increase inspections of wildlife and other imports into the country. More money also should be invested in basic research so that we understand how and why exotic species are successful. Additional funds need to be spent on biological control and other technologies that will reduce the damage that biological invaders cause.

Government agencies and conservation groups can also do more to stop biological invasions by communicating better with each other and by coordinating their efforts. Some states have already begun to cooperate, especially in dealing with aquatic pests. The Great Lakes Fishery Commission and the Colorado River Fish and Wildlife Council are two examples where officials from different states get together to work out guidelines for exotic species releases, inspections, and permits. Hawaii's Alien Species Action Plan group is another instance of how widely different interests can work together to overcome problems. Hundreds of other opportunities for cooperation exist at federal, state, and local levels.

In many ways, however, the problem of biological invasions comes down to personal awareness and responsibility. We as individuals can do a lot. One of the biggest obstacles to stopping invaders is that most people still don't realize they are an issue. Each of us can help overcome this problem by educating our friends, parents, and classmates about exotic species and the need to control them. The back of this chapter lists a number of additional steps we can take to stop invaders and protect native species.

All of our actions pay off. Every effort we make contributes to the preservation of our health, economy, environment, and our future. Though we have lost a lot, we still have plenty left worth saving. The question we have to answer is: Do we want to leave future generations a planet that is healthier, has fewer pests, and is home to a richer community of living species? Or do we want to leave future generations at greater risk from disease, pests, and environmental disasters?

The answer may seem clear, but still, it is a choice that every one of us has to make.

WHAT YOU CAN DO

The issue of exotic species is a tough one. It's tough to understand and to solve. However, if you are interested in helping to prevent future biological invasions and protect native species, there are a number of simple steps you can take:

1. Tell your friends about the problem of biological invasions. Learn and point out exotic plants and animals living near you.

2. Urge your parents and friends to plant only native species in yards and gardens. Native plants are often easier to take care of than exotic species, and they give more food and shelter to native animals.

3. Make sure your cats and dogs are neutered or spayed so that they won't produce unwanted offspring, which eat native birds and other wildlife.

*This chaparral growing in the mountains of
southern California is only one of countless ecosystems
that need to be protected from exotic species.*

4. Never release fish, reptiles, or other exotic pets into the wild. Don't buy or accept a pet unless you are willing to take care of it properly for the rest of its life. Also, know what you are getting into. A baby snake can grow into a 6-meter (20-foot) giant within several years. Ask yourself whether you are going to want to take care of such a pet.

5. Never carry live plants or animals with you when you travel. These living organisms might seem harmless, but they may escape and turn into destructive pests when you reach your destination. Also never carry products that are made from living organisms unless they have been certified pest free.

6. Never send plant or animal products through the mail unless they have been certified pest free.

7. If you are traveling across borders or into another country, always fill out a declaration card when it is asked for. On the card, list all fruits, vegetables, or other prohibited items you may be carrying.

8. Scrub the soles of your shoes before you travel to other places or go hiking in sensitive natural areas. Also scrub them when you come back. Many seeds and eggs of exotic species are too small for us to notice, but hitchhike quite well on the bottoms of shoes.

9. Write to your senators, members of Congress, and other political leaders. Urge them to help pass stricter regulations on importing exotic species and releasing genetically engineered organisms.

source notes

CHAPTER TWO

1. McKnight, Bill N., ed., *Biological Pollution: The Control and Impact of Invasive Exotic Species* (Indianapolis: Indiana Academy of Sciences, 1993), p. 2.

2. U.S. Congress, Office of Technology Assessment, *Harmful Non-indigenous Species in the United States: Summary.* (Washington, D.C.: Government Printing Office, 1993), p. 79.

3. Bruce F. Coblentz, "Exotic Organisms: A Dilemma for Conservation Biology," *Conservation Biology,* Vol. 4(3) (Sept. 1990).

CHAPTER THREE

1. Daniel Simberloff, quoted in *Biological Invasions: A Global Perspective,* J. A. Drake et al., eds. (Chichester, N.Y.: Wiley, 1989), p. 72.

2. Simon Levin, quoted in Roger Lewin, "Ecological Invasions Offer Opportunities," *Science,* Vol. 238 (Nov. 6, 1987), pp. 752–53.

3. Sir Frederick McMaster, landowner quoted in Eric C. Rolls, *They All Ran Wild: The Animals and Plants that Plague Australia* (Sydney: Angus & Robertson Publishers, 1969), p. 73.

CHAPTER FOUR

1. Robert V. Dowell and Raymond Gill, "Exotic Invertebrates and Their Effects on California." *Pan-Pacific Entomologist,* Vol. 65(2) (1989), 132–45.

2. Don Schmitz, Wetland and Upland Alien Plant Coordinator, Bureau of Aquatic Plant Management, Florida Department of Environmental Protection, quoted in Robert Devine, "Botanical Barbarians," *Sierra* (Jan/Feb 1994), p. 53.

3. Scott Johnson, Endangered Species Biologist, U.S. Fish and Wildlife Service, Honolulu, HI, interview with author, March 3, 1995.

CHAPTER FIVE

1. Edward O. Wilson, quoted in Charles C. Mann, "Fire Ants Parlay Their Queens Into a Threat to Biodiversity," *Science,* Vol. 263 (March 18, 1994), pp. 1560–61.

2. Alan Holt, Director of Science, The Nature Conservancy of Hawaii, Honolulu, HI, interview with author, March 9, 1995.

3. Patrick Conant, Entomologist, Hawaii Department of Agriculture, Honolulu, HI, interview with author, March 7, 1995.

4. Brian Cooke, Rabbit Calicivirus Disease Program team leader, quoted in a December 1, 1995 news release from Australia's CSIRO Division of Animal Health.

CHAPTER SIX

1. Art Medeiros, biologist, National Biological Service, interview with author, March 7, 1995.

2. Office of Technology Assessment, p. 11.

glossary

Acclimatization Societies—groups of colonists that worked to bring exotic species, usually from Europe, to such colonial territories as New Zealand and Australia.

agriculture—the science or practice of producing food or other useful products that consist of or come from other living things. Includes such activities as farming, cattle raising, aquaculture, timber raising, and horticulture.

AIDS—Auto-Immuno Deficiency Syndrome, a deadly disease usually spread through sexual contact, sharing hypodermic needles, or other direct contact with blood. AIDS is caused by a virus called HIV, or human immunodeficiency virus.

alien species—another name for exotic species.

APHIS—Animal and Plant Health Inspection Service,

a branch of the U.S. Department of Agriculture responsible for preventing the spread of pests and diseases that might affect agriculture.

aquaculture—the practice of raising aquatic plants and animals for food and other human uses. Shrimp and fish are common aquaculture crops.

ballast—water, dirt, rocks, or other heavy material that is placed in the holds of ships to help give them greater stability, especially when they are empty.

bandicoot—any of several kinds of small Australian marsupials that eat insects or vegetation.

biological control (biocontrol)—using one species to control or eradicate another species that is causing problems. Ladybird beetles are an effective biological control agent for controlling insect scale on citrus trees.

biological invader—any exotic organism that has become or is spreading through or has become established in a new habitat or region.

biological invasion—a case in which an exotic organism is actively becoming established in a habitat or region outside of its natural range.

biomass—the total weight of living organisms in a particular habitat or a particular ecological category in that habitat, for example the biomass of trees in a forest.

chaparral—a kind of ecosystem found in dry, warm,

coastal climates such as California, Mexico, and the Mediterranean basin. This ecosystem is dominated by evergreen shrubs and trees that grow well in dry, warm climates.

colonist—someone who settles in a new land or country. The term usually refers to Europeans who conquered and/or settled in such lands as New Zealand, Australia, Africa, Asia, and the Americas. A colonist can also be a plant or animal that settles in a new place.

competition—a situation in which a species must battle other species for food, water, light, or other natural resources.

dingo—a type of wild dog native to Australia. The dingo is one of the few Australian mammals that is not a marsupial.

Down Under—slang for Australia and sometimes New Zealand, lands in the southern hemisphere.

ecosystem—all of the living and nonliving parts of a place in nature. Ecosystems can be in land, air, and water. Examples of ecosystems are rain forests, ponds, deserts, and mountains.

emu—a large flightless bird native to Australia. Adult emus stand up to 2 meters (6 feet) tall.

encephalitis—swelling of the brain, usually caused by a parasitic diseases such as EEE, eastern equine encephalitis, a disease transmitted by mosquitoes.

entomology—the study of insects.

environment—all of the surroundings of an organism, including other living things, climate, and soils.

epidemic—an outbreak of a disease, such as measles or smallpox.

eradicate—to totally get rid of something, such as a population of exotic species.

evolution—the natural process by which new species change or are created.

exotic species—a plant, animal, or other species that is living outside of its natural range. Also called alien species or non-indigenous species.

extinction—the death or destruction of every individual in the population of a species.

feral—domestic pets, livestock, or other animals that are living and breeding freely in the wild. Cats and dogs are common feral animals that prey on native birds and other animals.

generalist—a species that can survive in many different kinds of habitats and conditions. Examples: rats, rabbits, and a number of weedy plants.

genetically engineered organism (GEO)—any living organism that has had genetic material from another species artificially incorporated into its own genetic material.

Gondwanaland—an ancient super-continent composed of a number of different tectonic plates. Geologists believe that the tectonic plates of Gondwanaland began drifting apart millions of years ago to form present-day South America, Africa, part of India, Australia, Antarctica, and New Zealand.

habitat disturbance—any action or event that disrupts or alters a natural community or place, including hunting, pollution, logging, grazing and so forth.

habitat—the environment in which an organism or population of organisms lives. A cold stream is the habitat of a trout.

histoplasmosis—a disease caused by a fungus that usually affects the respiratory system of mammals, including humans.

honeycreepers—a group of about forty species of native Hawaiian birds. Scientists believe that all honeycreepers evolved from a single kind of finch.

hybridization—the combining of two different species into a totally new species. Usually refers to plants.

introduced species—an exotic species, usually one that has purposely been brought to a new place. Rabbits in Australia are an introduced species.

larvae—the early forms or stages of animals that grow into several different forms during their lives. Mussels, clams, and many other aquatic animals begin their lives as tiny larvae that swim or float in the water. After they settle on the bottom or another surface, they change into the adult forms.

Latin America—the countries of South America, Central America, Mexico, and parts of the Caribbean.

marsupials—mammals—including kangaroos, wombats, and koala bears—in which the young develop in a special pouch instead of in a womb. Most marsupials are found in Australia, though some such as the opossum are found in other parts of the world.

mongoose—a small, weasel-like predator imported to Hawaii and other places to eat rats. Usually, mongooses have ended up eating native birds instead.

myxomatosis—a virus that is deadly to European rabbits. It has been used as a biological control agent in Australia and elsewhere.

naturalized—exotic organisms that have become permanently established in a new place and have been living there for many years.

Natural Resources Conservation Service—a branch of the U.S. Department of Agriculture that has traditionally worked to solved the problems of farmers and ranchers. One of their main activities has been to find plants, including exotic species, that help prevent soil erosion. Formerly known as the Soil Conservation Service or SCS.

New World—lands found in the western hemisphere, especially North and South America. The term refers to "new" lands discovered by Colombus and later explorers.

non-indigenous species—another name for exotic species.

Old World—lands found in the eastern hemisphere including Africa, Asia, Europe, and the Middle East.

organism—any individual living thing. Can be a plant, animal, virus, fungus, bacterium, or other life form.

OTA—The U.S. Congress Office of Technology Assessment. OTA prepared the 1993 report *Harmful Non-Indigenous Species in the United States.*

pandemic—an epidemic that affects a very large area or large proportion of a population. AIDS is a pandemic that affects almost every country in the world.

parasite—an organism that lives on or in another organism and usually survives by feeding off of its host. Mosquitoes are parasites that survive by drinking blood of humans and other animals.

plague—a contagious, often fatal, disease caused by a bacterium. A famous example is bubonic plague, also known as the Black Death.

Polynesians—native people of the western and central Pacific Ocean. Includes New Zealand's Maoris, native Hawaiians, and inhabitants of many other Pacific island groups.

predator—an animal that eats other animals.

quarantine—the process of isolating and sometimes treating plants, animals, or other things that may be carrying harmful diseases or pests.

rabbit calicivirus—a virus that has killed millions of rabbits in Asia, Europe, and elsewhere. It is now being used as a biocontrol agent to reduce Australian rabbit populations.

SCS—see Natural Resources Conservation Service.

semi-tropical—a climate that usually receives warm weather and extensive sunshine all year round, but may also experience brief spells of cooler weather. Florida and southern California are semi-tropical environments.

southern continent—another name for Australia.

swarm—a large colony of insects, such as African bees. Also means the process by which large groups of insects spread out and invade new territory.

transgenic organism—same as "genetically engineered organism."

USDA—United States Department of Agriculture.

wallaby—an Australian marsupial similar to a kangaroo.

weed—any undesirable plant species, especially those that compete with crop plants or interfere with human activities. Weeds usually reproduce very rapidly and thrive on disturbed sites such as fields and forest clearings.

wetlands—swamps, marshes, and other areas where the soil contains a lot of moisture during most parts of the year.

wombat—a marsupial about the size of raccoon. It is native to Australia and known for the burrows that it digs, which are also popular homes for introduced rabbits.

for further reading

The subject of biological invasions has received far less attention than many other environmental and social problems. Several good books, however, are available on the subject. *Immigrant Killers: Introduced Predators and the Conservation of Birds in New Zealand* by Carolyn M. King (Oxford University Press, 1984) gives an excellent history of the invasion of New Zealand by alien species. *Harmful Non-indigenous Species in the United States,* published by the U.S. Congress of Technology Assessment (1993) likewise gives a very up-to-date summary of the problem of exotic species in the United States. *They All Ran Wild: The Animals and Plants that Plague Australia* by Eric Rolls (Angus & Robertson Publishers, 1969) is a readable account of introduced species Down Under, including the European rabbit.

For additional information on rats, try *More Cunning Than Man: A Social History of Rats and Men* by Robert Hendrickson (Stein and Day Publishers, 1983). *Killer Bees* by Laurence Pringle (William Morrow,

1990), a young-adult title, provides an engaging introduction to African bees. *The Hot Zone* by Richard Preston (Random House, 1994) presents a riveting narrative of the emergence and first outbreaks of the ebola family of viruses while *Cane Toads, An Unnatural History* by Stephanie Lewis (Dolphin/Doubleday Press, 1989) takes a humorous look at the very real disaster produced by the introduction of cane toads into Australia.

For general references on the protection of biodiversity and the environment, also try the following books:

Langone, John J. *Our Endangered Earth: Our Fragile Environment & What We Can Do About It* (Boston: Little, Brown, 1992). [Young-adult title]

Middleton, Nick. *Atlas of Environmental Issues* (New York: Facts On File, 1989).

Pringle, Laurence. *Living Treasures: Saving Earth's Threatened Biodiversity* (New York: William Morrow, 1991).

Wilson, Edward O. *The Diversity of Life* (Cambridge, MA: Harvard University Press, 1992).

about the author

Sneed B. Collard III lives in Santa Barbara, California. He is the author of *Sea Snakes, Do They Scare You? Creepy Creatures,* and *Our Natural Homes: Exploring Terrestrial Biomes of North and South America.* When he is not writing, he spends much of his time speaking to students about nature and environmental protection.

acknowledgments

The author wishes to thank the following people for providing information, ideas, insights, and encouragment for this book.

Eldon E. Ball, Australian National University
Stan Bissell, California Department of Health Services
Debi Bogi, Michigan Sea Grant
    Communications Office
P.A. Butler, World Health Organization
Niall Byrne, Australian Animal Health Laboratory
Patrick Conant, Hawaii Department of Agriculture
Kevin Conner, U.S. Department of Agriculture
Sally Davis, California Exotic Pest Plant Council
Marion Dean, United States Fish and Wildlife Service
Robert V. Dowell, California Department of
    Food and Agriculture
Robert Gillmor, Artist
Chrissie Goldrick, State Library of New South Wales
Ken Hasegan, California Department of Fish and Game
Alan Holt, The Nature Conservancy of Hawaii

Scott M. Johnston, U.S. Fish and Wildlife Service
Lester Kaichi, Hawaii Department of Agriculture
Todd Kikuta, Hawaii Department of Agriculture
Homer Leong, United States Department
    of Agriculture
Lloyd Loope, National Biological Service
Barbara Maxfield, U.S. Fish and Wildlife Service
Cal McCluskey, U.S. Bureau of Land Management
Art Medeiros, National Biological Service
Harold A. Mooney, Stanford University
Tim Ohashi, United States Department of Agriculture
Don Parker, City of Oakland Fire Deptartment
Jane Rissler, Union of Concerned Scientists
Ronald W. Schlorff, California Deptartment of
    Fish and Game
Don C. Schmitz, Florida Department of
    Environmental Protection
Ron Schultze, United States Department
    of Agriculture
Jake Sigg, The California Native Plant Society
Emma Suarez, California Department of
    Food and Agriculture
Donna Weathers, California Department of
    Food and Agriculture
Jim White, United States Department of Agriculture

A special thanks to Susan Bartoletti, Sneed B. Collard Jr., Patrick Conant, Alan Holt, Lloyd Loope, Art Medeiros, and Harold Mooney for reviewing the manuscript and to Homer Leong for the great "plate" and my first glimpse of Pipeline.

index